Copies of the Guide can be obtained for $250 by calling (212) 303-3234.

TABLE OF CONTENTS

Page

INTRODUCTION

As derivatives products and strategies have grown in the past few years both in number and complexity, market professionals have increasingly bemoaned the dearth of comprehensive reference material on the subject. It was with this in mind that Institutional Investor created **Derivatives Week** in 1992, and the response was enormous.

The *Learning Curve* is a key feature of the newsletter and a major factor in its success. A weekly tutorial designed for the new or potential user of derivatives, each *Learning Curve* reviews the mechanics and uses of various instruments and strategies. The *Learning Curve* is now essential reading not only for derivatives novices but also for seasoned professionals who want to keep abreast of the latest market developments.

This book is **DW**'s first compendium of *Learning Curves*. It includes 52 features which explain the inner workings of products ranging from simple interest rate swaps to step-up recovery floaters—in layman's terms with the aid of both text and charts. Each feature appeared in **DW** and was updated, revised and redesigned by its editors and production staff for publication in this book.

Special thanks go to Robert Clow, Lewis Knox, Paul O'Keeffe, Lyn Perlmuth, Janine Schultz and Andrew Sollinger for their editorial efforts and to Susan Drobney and Chel Dong for their work in all aspects of production.

Tom Lamont
Editor
Derivatives Week

OPTIONS, PART I

An option contract conveys the right to buy or sell a specific quantity of a physical or intangible asset at a specific price within a preset time period. An option gives the buyer of the contract the right rather than the obligation to exercise at the preset price. The seller—or writer—of the option is committed to deal if the buyer chooses. The buyer pays the seller a premium for this privilege.

Options can be contracts to buy or sell physical assets—such as 10,000 shares of a particular company's stock or 10,000 barrels of oil—or contracts on something less tangible such as an index of underlying stocks, a contract on the future price of something or the exchange of payments (a swap).

An option may be traded on an exchange, in which case the contract details, including the quantity of the underlying instrument represented by one option, will be standardized. Alternatively, it may be traded over the counter (OTC), where typically the writer, a bank or broker, tailors the product to the buyer's needs.

Key parameters of an option include the strike or exercise price at which the buyer may choose to take up the option, and the time both to expiry and during which it may be exercised. An American-style option is one that can be exercised at any time during its life, while a European-style option is one that can only be exercised on the expiry date.

According to the UBS Phillips & Drew Beginners Guide to Traded Options, all option strategies are simply combinations of one or more of four basic ideas: buying calls, buying puts, selling calls or selling puts. Someone who buys an option which gives the right to buy the underlying asset is said to be buying a call. If he buys the right to sell the underlying asset, this is known as buying a put. Therefore the purchaser of a call or put option is buying the

RETURNS ON BASIC OPTIONS STRATEGIES

VALUE AT EXPIRATION. STRIKE = 100, PREMIUM = 10

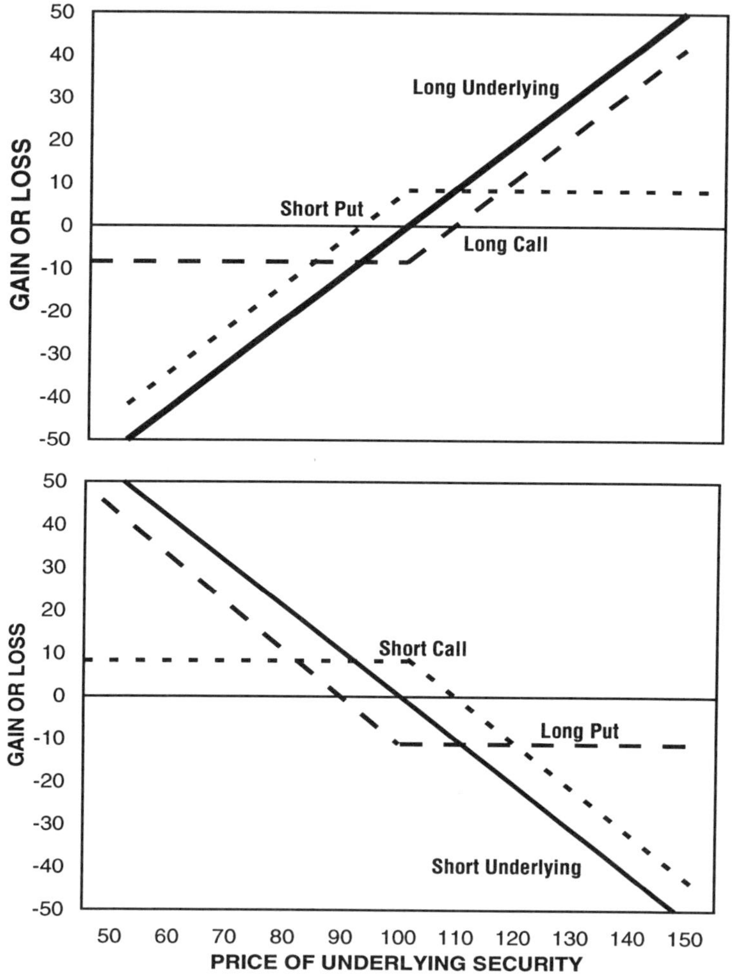

right to go long or short respectively of the underlying instrument. Either way his losses are limited to the premium he pays for this option while his profits are potentially unlimited.

The converse of these positions is the writer selling the right to buy, known as selling a call, or the right to sell, known as selling a put. The option writer's profits are therefore limited to the premium he receives while his losses are potentially unlimited if the buyer chooses to exercise the option.

> All option strategies are simply combinations of one or more of four basic ideas: buying calls, buying puts, selling calls or selling puts.

This limit on losses, for buyers, and profits, for sellers, is the obvious difference between an option and a future, according to the London International Financial Futures and Options Exchange (LIFFE). Since both the buyers and sellers of futures are committed to a transaction they both face potentially unlimited profits or losses.

Because the writer of options is exposing himself to potentially unlimited losses he may be required to put up a form of collateral called margin. The level of this, as well as the timing of when the buyer pays his premium, may vary from exchange to exchange to OTC deal.

Complex mathematical models like Black-Scholes are used in the theoretical pricing of options, though in the end price is determined by supply and demand, says GNI's head of research, Brian Durrant. The price can be split into two parts: intrinsic value and extrinsic or time value. Intrinsic value is the profit that could be made if the option were exercised immediately. It is the extent to which an option is "in the money". Extrinsic or time value reflects the option's time to expiry as well as the volatility of the underlying instrument.

There are a whole range of reasons for buying or selling puts and calls. Some of the most basic or common uses are:

- Buying calls to take advantage of any price increases in an underlying instrument without risking more than the premium.

- Buying puts to effectively insure against the fall in value of an underlying holding.
- Selling calls to generate income on existing underlying holdings (known as covered call writing).
- Selling puts, whether the writer owns the underlying instrument or not, to generate income, or at a strike price at which the writer would be happy to buy the underlying securities.

INTEREST RATE SWAPS

The essence of interest rate swaps is that they are exchanges of cash flows, according to Carolyn Jackson, v.p. and manager at Banque Indosuez in New York. In interest rate swaps, principal amounts do not change hands; it is just the interest payments that emanate from them that are exchanged.

Swaps came into existence because different types of borrowers enjoyed comparative advantages in different borrowing markets. John Shane, a v.p. in the capital markets group at Tokai Bank in New York, explains that one typical swap counterparty would be a manufacturer, who cannot borrow floating at as good a rate as fixed, and its opposite number might be an insurance company, which wants to receive fixed to pay annuities to its policy holders.

The problem was that counterparties often wanted to borrow in a market where they were at a disadvantage; corporations might have floating-rate liabilities, for example. In the late '70s financial institutions discovered a way to minimize the extra cost borrowers had to pay in less favorable markets by acting as middlemen, finding borrowers with different comparative advantages and different funding needs and matching them up as swap counterparties. Gradually, this system gave way to today's system where one counterparty is, almost inevitably, a financial institution.

In today's typical transaction, a bank might pay a corporation a floating rate, based on LIBOR or another index, and the bank might receive a fixed rate based on a government security yield with a swap spread added. Both parties win: the corporation is able to borrow floating at a competitive rate and the bank gets a higher return than it would from a standard risk-free investment.

The swap spread will be determined by the financial strength of the counterparty and the maturity and size of the swap. Financial institutions also put a value on their own creditworthiness, so a triple-A bank will charge more for its swap services than a lower-rated institution. But even in the event of default, swap counterparties have only a limited amount to lose. Because principal has not been exchanged, the risk is equal to the amount of the cash flow or the additional cost of replacing it.

Torsten Hinrichs, head of treasury at Westdeutsche Landesbank Europa in Dusseldorf, focused on six major advantages of swap transactions:

- They allow corporations to manage their interest rate exposure. In a rising interest rate environment it pays corporations to lock into a fixed rate while rates are still low. Conversely in a falling interest rate environment a swap can allow a corporation to pay floating and take advantage of falling rates.
- They provide a valuable tool for managing interest income. If

FLOATING FOR FIXED SWAP

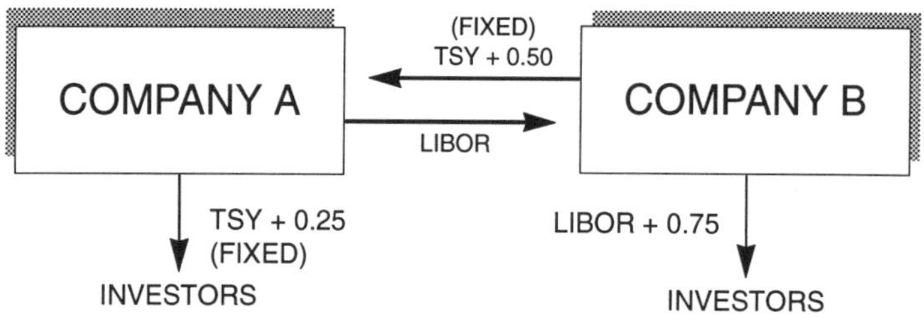

	BOND	SWAP	NET
COMPANY A (AAA)	-(TSY + 0.25)	-LIBOR +TSY + 0.50	-(LIBOR - 0.25)
COMPANY B (BBB)	-(LIBOR + 0.75)	-(TSY + 0.50) +LIBOR	-(TSY + 1.25)

Source: *Westdeutsche Landesbank*

a pension fund manager is receiving a floating rate on his investments, but he fears rates will fall, he can swap into a fixed rate.

• Swaps can be used to minimize borrowing costs, allowing counterparties to pay a lower rate than they could achieve in any other market. For example, in the accompanying diagram, Company A might be able to borrow at a fixed rate of the Treasury yield plus 25 basis points or at a LIBOR floating rate. But Company B, with a lower credit-rating, might only be able to borrow fixed at Treasury plus 150 basis points or floating at LIBOR plus 75 basis points. Company A could use its comparative advantage by borrowing fixed, while Company B could borrow floating. If A paid LIBOR to B and B paid Treasury plus 50 basis points in return in a floating-to-fixed swap, A could achieve a sub-LIBOR net borrowing cost and B would only have to pay Treasury plus 125 basis points for its fixed-rate borrowing.

> Swaps help manage interest rate exposure, interest income and borrowing costs.

• Using a swap, a company can access markets that would normally be closed to it. It might be able to borrow at a floating rate for 10 years, but only two years at a fixed rate. But if the company borrows floating for 10 years and swaps into fixed it can lock in a long-term fixed rate borrowing.

• Swaps can provide a cheap and efficient method of debt restructuring. If rates are rising, a company with floating-rate debt can lock in a fixed rate by paying fixed and receiving floating, thereby avoiding the transaction costs of refinancing the floating debt with fixed-rate instruments.

• Swaps have the advantage of liquidity. An active secondary market for swaps has developed so they can be undone quickly with a second, offsetting swap or assigned to another counterparty with a standard International Swaps and Derivatives Association (ISDA) form.

FUTURES CONTRACTS

A futures contract is an agreement between two parties, committing one to sell and the other to buy a specific quantity and quality of an instrument during some future delivery month or on some future date, according to Mike Stone, head of futures and options at Midland Global Futures. It is a legally binding standardized agreement traded on an exchange. The parties agree to buy or sell at a specific price in the future, and their profit or loss is determined by the difference between the arranged price and level of the spot price at expiry.

Contracts are physically deliverable or settled in cash, depending on the underlying instrument. A tangible underlying, such as copper, will often be physically deliverable, while cash-settled futures will be based on an instrument which would be impractical to deliver, for instance the FT-SE 100 stock index. The date and time of delivery will alter depending on the standardized agreement, but may occur on a certain day in a delivery month, or on any day during a specified month.

Taking the example of LIFFE's contracts, futures are three months in duration and traded in "delivery cycles." For instance, LIFFE lists four months at one time for its contracts in a March, June, September, December cycle. Once the "front-month," for example the December 1993 contract, has expired, the March 1994 contract takes its place and December 1994 will be added to ensure four months are always listed.

Buying a future involves paying an initial margin to the clearing house to provide collateral for the trade. Thereafter all open positions are re-valued on a marked-to-market basis and a variation margin is paid daily on that day's change in position. Margins are paid to the clearing house, the London Clearing House (LCH) in the case of London's exchanges, via a clearing member. LCH becomes the counterparty to all trades, eradicating credit risk as its major shareholders are the U.K.'s six major clearing banks.

Futures are priced by considering the current price of the underlying instrument and the opportunity gain or loss of holding the futures contract to maturity. That is:

Futures price = Spot + (opportunity costs - opportunity losses)

And it follows, because the opportunity cost of holding the future is related to time, that the price of the future, the "fair value," will move toward the price of the underlying instrument as the contract nears maturity.

In its guide to FT-SE 100 index futures, LIFFE points out that in practice the actual price of a futures contract will not be identical to its fair value because transaction costs in the underlying market, in this case equities, will create a band around which the future will trade. Often then, the trading price of a futures contract will differ

THEORETICAL VALUE VS CRUDE BASIS, MARCH 1992 FT-SE 100 INDEX FUTURE

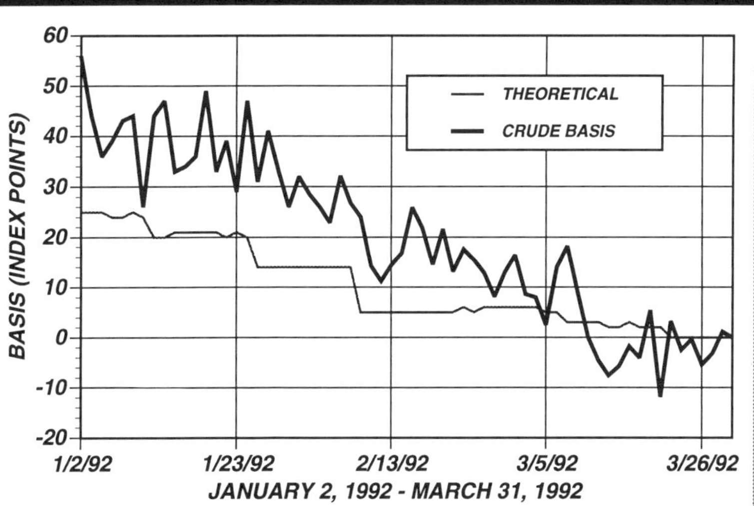

from its fair value price, and this difference is called the value basis.

When the value basis of a particular trading month is positive, that is, when the fair value is greater than the trading price, the futures contracts appear comparatively cheap, making that trading month attractive to buyers of the future.

Profit from an outright futures position depends on the directional moves of the underlying market, and because futures contracts carry the obligation to buy or sell the underlying instrument—unlike options, which convey rights, rather than obligations—the potential profits and losses are unlimited.

The difference between the price of the underlying and the fair value futures price is the theoretical value. Opportunities for arbitrage, a popular futures trading strategy, arise when the theoretical value differs from the crude basis, which is the difference between the underlying price and the futures trading price. Arbitrageurs buy (or sell) a futures contract and simultaneously take an equal and opposite position to profit from the mispriced contract months.

Profit from an outright futures position depends on the directional moves of the underlying market, and because futures contracts carry the obligation to buy or sell the underlying instrument—unlike options, which convey rights, rather than obligations—the potential profits and losses are unlimited. For instance, the CME Futures & Options Strategy Charts show that for a long futures position, profits increase without limit as the market rises.

Conversely, a short futures position is profitable if the market falls, and exposes the holder to unlimited losses if the market rises. The CME charts point out that futures positions are beneficial for traders with definite bullish (long) or bearish (short) views, but without views on volatility. When traders have definite views about volatility, which are proved correct, an options position may be more appropriate as this can limit the downside risk, and enhance

OPTIONS, PART II

Each of the four basic option strategies—buying and selling calls and buying and selling puts—might be used to meet a range of objectives.

Buying calls:

• To take advantage of price increases in the underlying instrument without risking more than a premium.

• For geared exposure to an underlying price. This is because, on a percentage basis, an option's price is more sensitive than that of the underlying, according to Nick Maggs, training manager at the International Petroleum Exchange in London. "It is easier to gain 100% on the option premium than on the physical," he said. The more bullish you are, the more out-of-the-money (the higher the strike price is above the price of the underlying) should be the call you buy, says the Chicago Mercantile Exchange Futures & Options Strategy Charts.

• To defer a decision to buy the underlying during a period of price uncertainty but retaining the exposure to any upside movement in price.

• To help cash flow or to anticipate an inflow of funds. As a substitute for buying the underlying, a call option also offers a notional saving on interest.

• As a hedge. An investor who is bearish about the underlying can sell the physical but guard against a rise in price by buying a call.

Buying puts:

• To insure against a fall in the price of an underlying holding, i.e., as a hedge.

● Related to the above, to defer a decision on when to sell the underlying. Perhaps the holder thinks there is a chance that prices will increase, offering him a better sale price if he hangs on, but he also wants to protect against a fall in price in the interim.

● To gear exposure to an underlying price movement, just as with calls, but in this case on the downside. If the price of the underlying rises, the put buyer does not exercise the option and his losses are limited to the original premium.The more bearish the put buyer is, the more out-of-the-money should be the put, suggests the CME.

Selling calls:

● To generate income on existing holdings, sometimes described as performance enhancement. The risk for the call seller is that he will have to sell the underlying at less than the market price. Invesco MIM equity fund managers typically sell covered calls after a stock has had a good run and then looks as though it is sta-

RETURNS ON SHORT CALL POSITIONS AT EXPIRATION

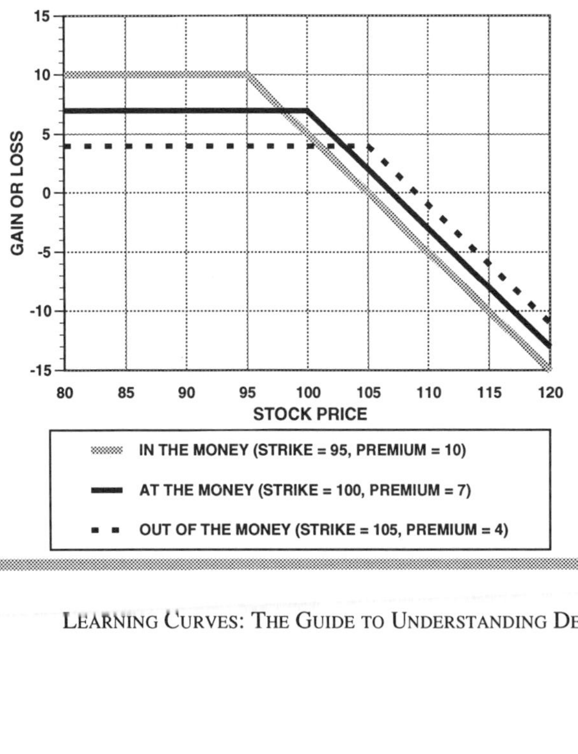

bilizing, said Stephen Fitzgerald, senior portfolio manager in London.

• When the investor does not hold the underlying, he may speculate the price will not rise dramatically by selling a call (see graph). In this case he is taking income but bears the risk of potentially unlimited losses. If he thinks there is a chance the market will rise he should sell out-of-the-money calls, the CME suggests. On the other hand if he is very confident the underlying will stagnate or fall, he should sell at-the-money calls. And if he doubts it will even stagnate, rather than just fall, he should sell in-the-money calls for maximum premium profit, it says.

> The equivalent strategy to buying a put is to sell the underlying and buy the call. The equivalent to selling a call is to sell the stock and sell the put, while the equivalent of selling the put is to buy the stock and then sell the call.

Selling puts:

• To generate income while being prepared to buy the underlying at the agreed strike price. Put sellers might think there is little chance of the price of the underlying falling to the strike level, but if it does they are not worried about buying it at that price.

• To speculate that the underlying price will not fall. But if a put seller thinks there is a chance the underlying price will fall he should sell out-of-the-money puts, the CME suggests. Conversely, if he is very confident it will stagnate or rise, he should sell puts at or even in the money.

The risk profiles of each of these strategies can be recreated using combinations of stocks and options, according to a UBS Phillips & Drew publication, A Compendium of Option Strategies. The equivalent risk strategy to buying a call is to buy the underlying and buy the put, says UBS. Both offer unlimited profit. Losses on the call purchase are limited to the premium paid, while those on the alternative strategy are limited to the price paid for the underlying plus the premium paid, less the exercise price of the put, it says. Likewise, the equivalent strategy to buying a put is to sell the underlying and buy the call. The equivalent to selling a call is to sell the stock and sell the put, while the equivalent of selling the put is to buy the stock and sell the call, says UBS.

CAPS, FLOORS AND COLLARS

Caps and floors are options designed to hedge against interest rate moves. Caps hedge against rates moving up and floors protect holders from rates moving down. Dan Calacci, a v.p. at Sakura Global Capital Markets, says many buyers of caps today are floating-rate borrowers with ratings too low for them to be a swap counterparty. Swap players say that regional banks, with floating-rate assets on their balance sheets, are probably the biggest buyers of floors, but Calacci says it could be worthwhile for any company with large cash holdings to buy floors in a falling interest rate environment.

Caps and floors have strikes which are set against an index. If the index (for a cap) rises above or (for a floor) falls below the a given rate, the option seller will pay the difference. Mark Starr, v.p.-institutional marketing at Chase Manhattan Bank, says he bases caps on a number of indices. LIBOR is the most common, but he also uses the commercial paper and prime rates. Typically, a company might buy a cap at 10%, based on LIBOR, and if LIBOR rises above 10%, the seller will pay the difference between LIBOR and 10%. Conversely, a company buying a floor would receive the difference between the strike price and LIBOR, if LIBOR were lower than the strike.

Like other options, caps and floors are asymmetrical hedges. A cap or floor owner is protected against an adverse change in interest rates, but can still benefit from a move in his favor.

The pricing components of a cap or floor are the length of protection, the strike price, option volatility and the slope of the yield

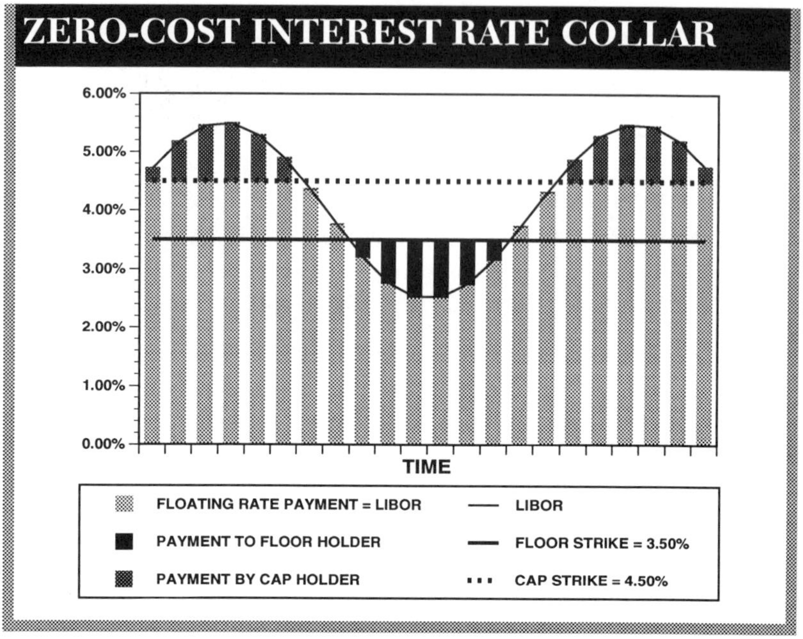

curve. The longer-dated options cost more; caps with lower strike prices and floors with higher strike prices are more expensive.

Sellers of caps or floors use Black-Scholes options models to compute implied volatility, which is defined as the percentage of a year when interest rates will be more than one standard deviation from where they are now. John Stomber, managing director-derivative products at Deutsche Bank Capital Corp., says implied volatilities are high at the moment because of the absolute level of interest rates, supply and demand factors and historical volatility. The absolute level of interest rates is important, he explains, because a 25-basis-point move when interest rates are at 4% will have a far more pronounced effect on volatility than a 25-basis-point move when rates are at 8%. Supply and demand for volatility from banks and broker/dealers bid up the price those institutions are willing to pay for it.

The slope of the yield curve is also important. A steep yield curve implies that rates will rise quickly and, as a result, caps could soon be in-the-money.

It is also possible to purchase a collar. This might entail buying a cap and selling a floor (see graph), or vice versa. The advantage of a collar is the low cost; the cost of the cap can be offset against the premium received from the floor. The disadvantage of buying a collar is that it limits the benefit of an interest rate move in the right direction.

CURRENCY FORWARDS, SWAPS AND OPTIONS

Currency forwards are contracts to exchange currency at a future point in time, says Ezra Zask, former head of global foreign exchange trading at Mellon Bank, now running his own firm out of Connecticut. The amount of currency and the time of exchange can be varied.

The price of a forward contract is made up of two components: the "spot" and "swap" rate (not to be confused with a currency swap or swap spread). The spot price is the exchange rate today; the swap rate is the amount the spot has to be adjusted to give a forward price. A rough formula for calculating the swap rate is:

$$\mathbf{S\ (ix\text{-}iy)\ T}$$

S is the spot rate; **ix** is the interest rate in the currency bought, **iy** the interest rate in the currency sold and **T** is the length of the contract, expressed as a fraction of a year. (This formula does not account for differences in the way interest rates are quoted in different markets.) In the U.S. foreign exchange market the swap rate is normally added to spot to give a forward rate. Commonwealth currency exchange rates, however, are quoted in reverse, showing how many dollars it will take to buy a pound, for example. This means the differential is subtracted from the spot to give a forward rate.

A company buying a three-month pound forward with the spot rate at 1.773 when U.K. interest rates were 10% and U.S. rates were 4% would pay a forward rate of 1.743, calculated as follows:

$$1.773\ (0.10 - 0.04)\ 0.25 = 0.03$$
$$1.773 - 0.03 = 1.743$$

As a rule of thumb, says David Durst, assistant v.p. of foreign exchange at Crédit Lyonnais, you add the swap where the other country has a higher interest rate than the home market and the exchange rate is quoted in the European style. As to when the currency is exchanged, Durst says no money changes hands until the contract is completed.

The forward market is huge and enormously liquid, but Durst and his colleagues find the market pretty illiquid for any time past a year, even in the major currencies. David Greenberg, v.p. in charge of marketing foreign exchange options at Banque Paribas, says this illiquidity can often be remedied by the swap desk.

DM/US$ 3 YEAR 6 MONTH LIBOR/ 6 MONTH LIBOR BASIS SWAP

Value Date	DM Borrower			Dollar Borrower	
	Implied LIBOR	Rate including spread	Payments to $ borrower	Implied LIBOR	Payments to DM borrower
May 19, 1992			DM16,800,000		$10,000,000
Nov. 19, 1992	9.81%	9.83%	$213,644	4.18%	DM844,069
May 19, 1993	9.21	9.23	$258,931	5.15	DM779,627
Nov. 19, 1993	8.65	8.67	$307,178	6.01	DM744,464
May 19, 1994	8.19	8.21	$348,928	6.94	DM693,471
Nov. 19, 1994	8.22	8.24	$376,178	7.36	DM707,541
May 19, 1995	7.99	8.01	$10,399,206	7.94	DM17,476,578

NOTES: Implied LIBORs were forecast by then-current market rates for the 6 month period up to each value date. The final cash flows include re-exchange of principal plus interest.

Source: ***Sanwa Financial Products***

Currency swaps are different from interest rate swaps in that they involve an exchange of principal. The different currencies are exchanged at the spot rate with an agreement to re-exchange at the same rate when the swap terminates, says Greenberg. In between these two exchanges, cash payments are made as though the swap was a series of forward contracts. Interest rate differentials are calculated by looking at the yield curves of different countries and forward rates are calculated from there. According to Zask, the only difference between calculating forward rates here and in the forward market is that interest rates are compounded—as they are in the Eurobond market.

Currency swaps are different from interest rate swaps in that they involve an exchange of principal.

Each counterparty pays interest in the currency into which it has swapped. If counterparty A borrows in DM and swaps into dollars with counterparty B, A will pay B dollar interest and B will pay A DM interest (see table). The reason for this, explains Burton Hilton, v.p. at Sanwa Financial Products, is that both parties retain their original borrowing liabilities. So A receives Deutsche marks with which to pay DM interest to its creditors and vice versa.

Spreads on currency swaps are quoted the same way as interest rate swaps—as a spread over a government or risk-free bond—and the spreads are determined the same way—looking at the maturity of the swap, the counterparty credit and the size of the deal. Originally currency swaps were all fixed-fixed, but now they can be fixed-floating or even floating-floating.

Currency options are also slightly different from other options; they have a dual nature. A call option on the pound, taken out on the pound/dollar exchange rate, could also accurately be described as a put on the dollar. But neither Durst nor Greenberg think this results in any difference in the way the market operates. Prices for currency options are calculated using the Black-Scholes model, with the exception that two interest rates are fed into the currency option formula. Unlike stock option pricing models, which take into account the difference between a dividend yield and a risk-free interest rate, currency models use the interest rate differential between the two currencies involved. Prices for options are quoted in the interbank market as volatilities while prices to customers are quoted as a percentage of the amount to be hedged.

BASIC OPTIONS PRICING

The theoretical price of an option is made up of two parts: intrinsic and extrinsic value. Intrinsic value is determined by the extent to which the strike price of the option is above or below the spot price—that is whether it is in or out of the money. But the extrinsic value is more difficult to determine as it is made up of a number of variable factors. This is what the first theoretical options pricing model, Black-Scholes, aimed to quantify by giving the variables, mainly the price of the underlying asset and the volatility with which price moves, known values.

The principle of uncertainty is the basis of any options pricing model, explains John Parry, a lecturer on derivatives markets and a partner in marketing consultancy Rostron Parry. How can an investor value an option if he does not know whether the underlying asset price will change so that the option moves into the money in the future? Black-Scholes turns to random walk theory for the answer: it assumes that the underlying asset price is as likely to rise as it is to fall. This is a critical assumption of the Black-Scholes model and quantifies one of the potential unknowns—the underlying asset price is assumed to follow a lognormal distribution during the life of the option.

But it is simpler to turn to binominal models such as that developed by Cox, Ross and Rubenstein, developed soon after Black-Scholes, to understand the reasoning behind the assumptions about the distribution of returns on the underlying assets, explains Sam Armstrong, with Swiss Bank Corp. in Sydney. The Cox-Ross-

Rubenstein pricing model describes the distribution of possible future prices during the lifetime of the option by considering the possible movements of the underlying asset price at different points in time by using a binominal distribution to construct a probability tree.

Cox-Ross-Rubenstein assumes that the price of the underlying asset can follow any one of the paths along the tree (see figure). For instance, in the first period the price may go up or down and in the next period, assuming the stock price went up, it may then go up or down, and so the tree is constructed. The option value at each node in the tree is calculated by multiplying the probability of arriving at that node by the stock price, Armstrong said. The probability that the price will move up or down is attributed to each branch of the tree, so the chance of arriving at any node is equal to the probability raised to the power of the number of periods. The price of the option is reached by following those branches of the tree which show that the option is in the money, and summing the results together.

COX-ROSS-RUBENSTEIN OPTIONS PRICING MODEL

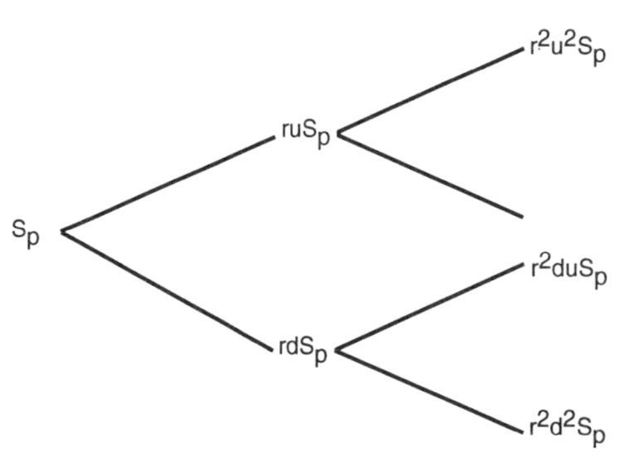

S_p = current stock price
r = probability of moving up or down
u =1+ fractional increase
d =1- fractional decrease

Determining the probability with which an option will finish in the money is also the basis of the Black-Scholes model, Armstrong says, as the price of the option is determined by multiplying the spot price by the probability that the option will finish in the money. In determining that probability the great unknown variable is volatility, explains Armstrong. Essentially, the higher the volatility the more expensive the option, because as volatility rises, so does the chance that the option will finish in the money.

> The higher the volatility the more expensive the option, because as volatility rises, so does the chance that the option will finish in the money.

Black-Scholes assumes volatility is at a constant level and can be measured through standard deviations of historical prices. But, explains Armstrong, this simplistic view is now adapted by many options professionals to more sophisticated measures, so that more recent historical data, say for the last year, is given more weight than data from three years ago. Other volatility measures involve forming projections of volatility, called volatility cones, into the future.

The option's time to expiration is another facet in the Black-Scholes model. Armstrong explains that the Black-Scholes model assumes that the price of the option is related to the square root of time. The longer the life of the option, the more expensive it will be, says Armstrong, as the chances of the option finishing in the money will increase.

The last main component, interest rates, enters into the Black-Scholes model as an opportunity cost, according to Parry, and the higher the interest rate, the higher the price of the option. This follows from the assumption that a stock option writer, for instance, will be using cash to hold the underlying asset and not placing the cash on deposit and gaining interest. The higher the interest rate the greater the opportunity cost of writing the option. From an option buyer's point of view, when interest rates are high the more likely the buyer is to keep cash on deposit than buying the underlying stocks, and so will buy an option at a higher price to gain exposure to the market.

The Black-Scholes model did not make any allowance for dividend payments from stocks, explains Armstrong, and subsequent options pricing models have aimed to handle dividends. Black-Scholes also concentrated on European-style options, which cannot be exercised before maturity, although Armstrong explains that the model still holds for American-style calls where there are no dividends as they are rarely exercised early.

MORTGAGE SWAPS AND MORTGAGE HEDGING TOOLS

Mortgage-linked derivative products are synthetic mortgages which can be kept off-balance sheet or swaps which can hedge against the extension or reinvestment risk stemming from changing prepayment levels.

Mortgage products have become especially important, as mortgages have outperformed Treasuries in many cases and low interest rates have created high prepayment levels. Most U.S. residential mortgages are based on a fixed rate, so lower rates can spark a wave of refinancing. When this takes place, existing mortgages are paid down, thereby increasing prepayment levels, and new ones are taken out at lower fixed rates.

According to investment banks, mortgage-like products have created the biggest demand. These are usually amortizing swaps: interest rate swaps with a notional principal which declines (thus reducing payments) according to a predetermined schedule. In a typical mortgage swap, the swap house pays the mortgage-based return while its customer pays a floating rate. The amortization schedule on the swap can be identical to the prepayment rate on an underlying mortgage pool or the schedule can be tied to an index. According to Joseph Brennan, managing director at Sumitomo Bank Capital Markets, banks and financial institutions buy these synthetic mortgages because, unlike the real thing, they can take them off-balance sheet and, as a result, they do not need to make as large a capital provision against them.

In the second type of amortizing mortgage swap, the amortization schedule varies according to LIBOR or CMT (constant maturity Treasury) or any other interest-rate benchmark. In those cases, the client might set the parameters for the deal. He might, for instance, set a five-year target for a $100 million notional amount to amortize and set a seven-year maximum range. Frequently, the swap will not start amortizing until it is one-third into its life, thus mimicking some collateralized mortgage obligation tranches. According to the head of one U.S. swaps desk, CMT swaps and CMT caps and floors are particularly popular when mortgage prepayment levels are more closely correlated to Treasury yields than LIBOR; CMT instruments eliminate some of the basis risk.

Amortizing swaps can be used to take a view on the yield curve because an investor receiving fixed would be receiving a high interest rate based on implied LIBOR. In addition, the

CASH FLOWS IN AN AMORTIZING SWAP

PERIOD	FWD LIBOR (%)	AMORTIZATION SCHEDULE (%)	NET CASH FLOWS
1	3.92	100.00	$347,353
2	4.22	100.00	300,892
3	4.79	100.00	158,608
4	5.14	42.67	30,452
5	5.55	28.88	(7,490)
6	6.03	22.39	(30,980)
7	6.57	19.79	(54,836)
8	6.82	18.11	(53,609)
9	7.02	17.02	(60,120)
10	7.28	16.55	(69,480)

NOTES: Amortization schedule is calculated assuming zero volatility. Net cash flows represent the present value of payoffs to a 5.5% fixed-rate receiver.

Source: ***Sumitomo Bank Capital Markets***

fixed receiver is selling interest rate volatility, so a yield curve which is very steep would put a high value on implied volatilities. The amortization schedule is based on the position of the yield curve today.

> Mortgage-linked derivative products are synthetic mortgages which can be kept off-balance sheet or swaps which can hedge against the extension or reinvestment risk stemming from changing prepayment levels.

The pricing for these deals is based on the same factors as that of an interest rate swap but there is an element of optionality in these deals because, at the time of pricing, the direction and pace of changes in interest rates are unknowns. This uncertainty is factored into the price using Monte Carlo simulations, which run a large number of possible interest-rate scenarios and then average out the prepayment levels and costs.

A mortgage swap tied to an index, sometimes called a "rate of return" swap, is very similar to the synthetic mortgage products except that, rather than paying based on the amortization of a particular mortgage-backed security, a mortgage swap pays a rate based on the Salomon Mortgage Index or the mortgage portion of the Shearson Lehman Bond Index. A mortgage index swap allows users to earn a return based on mortgage-backed securities without taking a view on any particular mortgage instrument or group of instruments.

In addition to these investment tools, there are also mortgage hedging tools. Some firms sell prepayment caps and floors to hedge against extension risk—when prepayments slow—or reinvestment risk, when they speed up. According to David Langer, v.p.-mortgage derivatives at BT Securities, these instruments compensate investors if their investment extends in duration and their cost of capital increases. If that happens, the option writer will make up the difference between the return on the mortgage and the investor's new cost of capital.

Alternatively, Langer says, prepayment options can be used to hedge against reinvestment risk, when mortgages are paying off too fast and an investor is forced to reinvest at a lower rate. In the latter case, the option writer will make up the difference between the lower reinvestment rate available to the mortgage holder and the rate the mortgage is paying.

One example of a shorter-term mortgage hedging tool is Goldman's MOTO (mortgage-over-Treasury) options or the Merrill Lynch equivalent. The underlying securities in that case could be the spread between any Treasuries and any mortgages. These options allow investors to hedge against the possibility of Treasuries outperforming mortgages and also against extension risk. According to John Coates, v.p. in charge of trading spread options at Goldman Sachs, an option writer can hedge against prepayment risk by taking the premium from an option and adding it to the return on his mortgage pool.

DELTA, GAMMA, VEGA AND THETA

An option's price is determined by a number of factors, and all these factors can change at once. To gauge how these variables will change the value of their positions, options traders have devised methods of measuring the effects of each of them on the options price, explains Mark Shipman, principal at Silver Knight Investment Management: Delta measures how much the premium will move in relation to a change in the underlying price; gamma is the rate at which delta changes; theta the effect on the premium of a change in time to expiry of the option; vega measures the effects of changes in volatility on the option price. David Brierwood, principal in international equity at Morgan Stanley International in London, says that longer-term strategists also look at rho, which represents the effect interest rates have on option premium.

Delta decreases toward 0 as the option moves out of the money and increases toward 1 when the option moves into the money, as the option begins to behave like the underlying asset, says Mike Hudson, principal at The Sunrise Company (see figure). If a trader is long the underlying asset his position has a positive delta; if the market rises the trader's position will gain in value. Should the market fall rapidly the position will be worth less.

Delta is mainly associated with dynamic hedging, also called delta hedging, Hudson explains. Hedgers by definition are not gaining or losing on their positions, and use delta to maintain a neutral position. For example, assume an index is at $100, and that a trader buys a one-year index call with a delta of +0.6 for $5. If the index moves up $1, the trader might expect the call to be worth $5 + ($1 x 0.6), or $5.60, Hudson says. This is not a hedged position as the trader has gained from a rise in the market.

As futures have a delta of +1.0, the trader may short 0.6 of a futures contract to bring delta back to zero. He is then delta-hedged. However, an option's delta changes as the price of the underlying asset changes and a delta-neutral position may become unhedged as the market moves. If the underlying rises to $101, the call option's delta might rise to +0.7. As the delta of the futures contract does not change with the underlying asset, the trader has net delta of +0.1. To regain delta neutrality the trader would short a further 0.1 of a futures contract.

Maintaining a delta-neutral options position in a moving underlying market involves frequent buying and selling of futures contracts, concludes Hudson. How quickly delta changes is measured by gamma; a gamma-neutral position need not be adjusted when the price of the underlying changes. The accompanying figure represents the delta of a call spread and a put spread, both construct-

DELTA AND GAMMA HEDGING

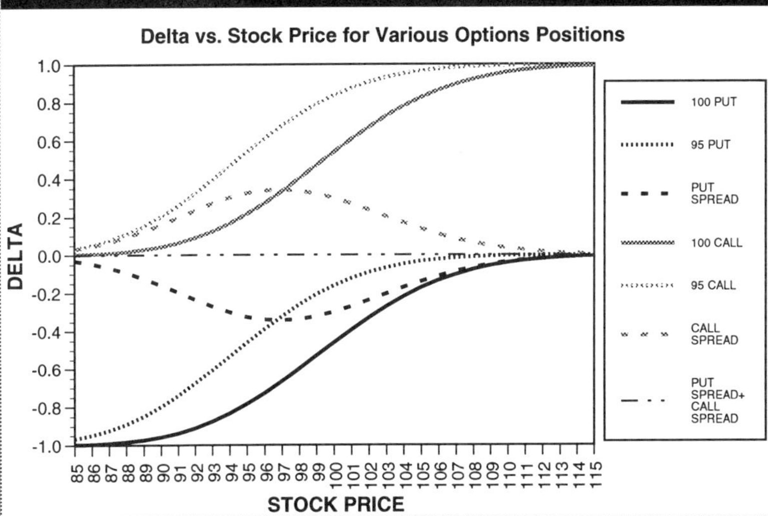

ed with the same strikes; the slope of the delta curves represent gamma. Note that the call spread's delta and gamma always offset the put spread's delta and gamma for any underlying asset price. As a result, a trader who owns both spreads is both delta- and gamma-hedged. This hedged position is commonly referred to as a "box."

A trader who owns both spreads is both delta- and gamma-hedged. This hedged position is commonly referred to as a "box."

Because futures have a constant delta, they have gamma of zero, so traders would gamma-hedge through combinations of options contracts. Brierwood points out that gamma can be seen as a measure of the stability of a delta hedge.

Closely related to gamma is vega, also known as kappa, says Brierwood. The main difference between the two is that vega measures the sensitivity of the option price to changes in the perception of future volatility, while gamma measures the actual rate of change in the delta with the price of the underlying. Brierwood points out that portfolio managers can create zero-vega positions, free of volatility risk, through such trades as being long stock, short calls and long puts.

Theta, the effect of a change in an option's lifespan on the price of the option, becomes more important as an option moves toward expiry because this is when its time value decreases at a faster rate than earlier in its life, explains Shipman. Options traders will use theta in time plays, when the underlying market is perceived to be static, because the strategy will gain from the depreciation associated with time. For example, an options trader may sell September calls and buy November calls, he explains. If the market does not move, the position will show profit on the shorter-dated options because of the increasing theta component in the price.

EQUITY INDEX SWAPS

Equity swaps can take a variety of forms, explains Alison Rich, until recently a principal at The Sunrise Company. The most common involve a swap between the return on a stock index and a benchmark rate of interest, usually LIBOR. There are two parties to equity index swaps, the index receiver and the interest rate receiver. Swaps can also involve the exchange of returns on two different indices, or more rarely involve the returns on a single stock against LIBOR, she adds.

Typically, a bank will pay the return on the index, and the client the rate of interest benchmark. Cash flows and settlements may take place on a monthly or quarterly basis or, in some cases, through a single payment at the end of the swap, depending on the agreement between the two counterparties. If the swap is against three-month LIBOR, for instance, then payments are most likely to take place quarterly, explains Rich.

One of the initial motivations behind equity index swaps was to allow portfolio managers prohibited from using futures contracts to gain exposure to markets where the futures contracts traded systematically cheap to fair value, says Timothy Keating, deputy managing director at Nomura International in London. In the process, portfolio managers not only get the required exposure to the market but also receive the return on an index, plus an additional payment of, say, 50 basis points (bp), including commissions and transaction costs, he adds.

Keating uses an example based on the DAX index to explain the cash flows and savings involved in the swap. He makes the following assumptions: the index level is 1732.18, annual dividend yields are 2.007%, or 34.77 index points for the period, and withholding tax on the dividends 15%. The swap is assumed to be 182 days, that is six months, and the initial value of the stock portfolio with accumulated dividends DM10,000,000. In the following example, he shows that the return on holding the underlying shares is reduced by the withholding tax, and that entering into a DAX swap offering 50 bp plus the return on the index would offer an incremental total return of 50 bp, and avoid the withholding tax.

Breaking down the returns from holding the underlying stock, Keating assumes that the cash from dividends will amount to DM200,713 (34.77 index points) but that the 15% withholding tax will cost the portfolio manager DM30,107. So, the value of the ex-dividend stocks is assumed to amount to DM9,799,287, but the overall value of the portfolio is DM9,969,893, which is the value of the initial portfolio, plus the cash dividends minus the withholding tax. In percentage terms, this shows a negative return of 0.3%, says Keating.

The portfolio manager would gain what Keating calls a "swap pickup" from entering into an equity swap in the same market con-

DAX INDEX SWAP

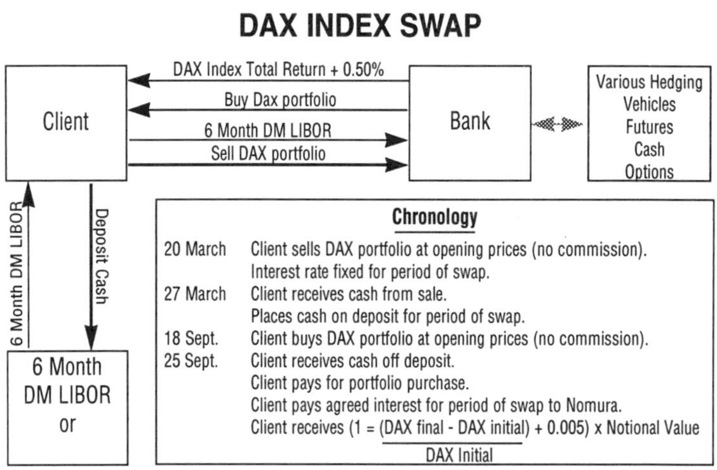

Source: ***Nomura International***

ditions. The portfolio manager would sell his DAX portfolio to the bank and deposit the cash he receives in an interest bearing account, typically receiving six-month DM LIBOR. In our example, this would amount to DM488,159, which the portfolio manager would pay to the bank at the end of the agreed six-month life of the swap (see figure), says Keating. The portfolio manager would correspondingly receive at the end of the six-month swap the total return on the DAX index plus the 50 bp agreed upon at the outset. He would then repurchase the DAX portfolio.

Equity swaps are useful asset allocation tools, especially for managers of index funds.

Banks agree to be index-return payers because it allows them to short the market less expensively than they could by borrowing shares. Nomura would avoid the withholding tax from the portfolio of stocks it bought by immediately moving out of the stocks and into the futures markets.

In Keating's example of the DAX, as 100% of the dividends from the stocks that compose the index are reinvested, the total return is zero. The portfolio manager has gained DM50,000, or 0.5%, on his portfolio during the life of the swap, and has not been subject to withholding tax. In comparison with holding stock, the manager has gained 0.8% (0.5% + 0.3%), concludes Keating.

Equity swaps are useful asset allocation tools, especially for managers of index funds, notes Ian Hall, first v.p. at Republic National Bank of New York in London. As physical shares are not exchanged, equity swaps allow easy exposure to any market. "Paying LIBOR against an index appeals to an index fund. They go out with the money and earn something linked to LIBOR. It's an alternative to buying stock," explains Hall.

Equity swaps may also be appealing because they avoid the administrative work involved in trading futures, explains Rich. To trade futures contracts, investors must make daily margin payments. Because swaps involve payment flows on a less regular basis, they carry fewer transaction costs.

STRADDLES AND STRANGLES

Straddles and strangles are strategies which involve the use of several options in concert. A straddle is created by buying or selling equal amounts of puts and calls with the same strike price, the same underlying and the same expiry. A strangle involves buying or selling puts and calls on the same underlying at different strike prices.

Both strategies are directionally neutral—the buyer or seller is generally indifferent as to which way the market moves—but the strategies provide ways to go long or short volatility. For example, buying a straddle that consists of an at-the-money put and an at-the-money call would be profitable if the underlying asset jumped (or fell) in price so dramatically that the profit on one side of the position offset the loss on the other, which is limited to the premiums paid in any case. A strangle buyer might go long out-of-the-money calls and out-of-the money puts (see figures). He wins under the same circumstances as the straddle buyer, except that the underlying would have to make a bigger move. Out-of-the-money options have a lower delta and therefore will appreciate more slowly for a given move in the underlying. On the other hand, the out-of-the-money options will have lower premiums than at-the-money contracts.

Buyers and sellers of straddles and strangles have very different motives, explained Harry Roth, first v.p. and sr. options strategist at Cowen & Co. Sellers rely on the market staying flat or relatively neutral. The buyers typically are expecting a large price move, but they are not sure which way the securities are going to move. Roth noted that a very volatile biotechnology stock might provide a good opportunity for the buyer of a strangle.

Mike Schwartz, senior v.p. and chief options strategist at Oppenheimer & Co., cautioned that there are not many times when it is a good idea to buy a straddle. The buyer is paying two option premiums, one for the put and one for the call. Thus, the straddle would be expensive and it might take a great deal of

STRANGLE (top) AND STRADDLE (bottom) VALUES AS A FUNCTION OF STOCK PRICE

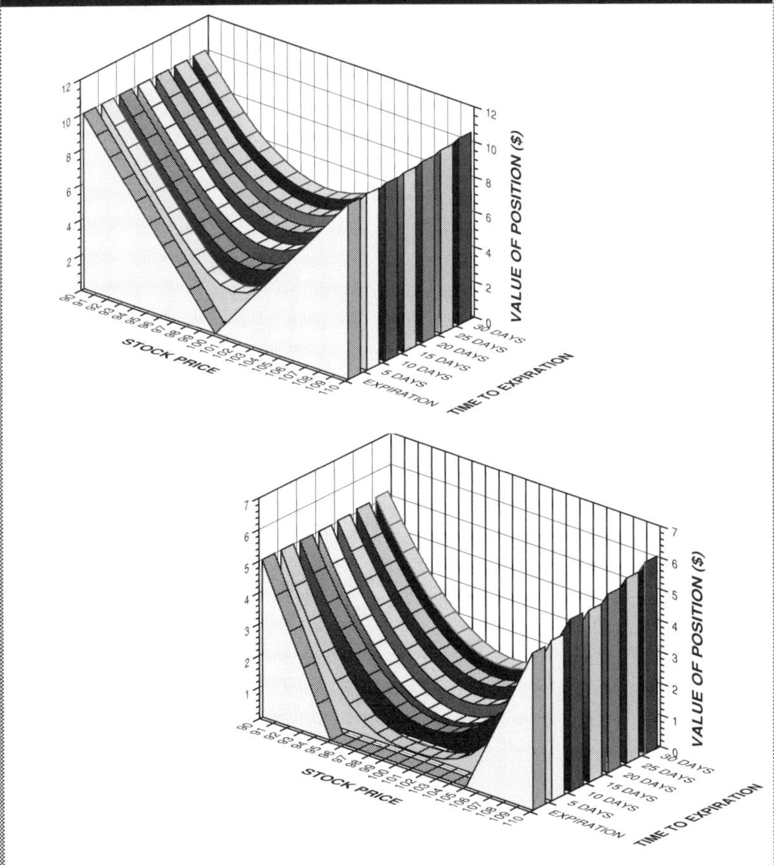

movement for the buyer to recoup the premium. Buying a strangle rather than a straddle would be one way to diminish the premium expense, Schwartz said. The buyer of a strangle will still have to pay two premiums, but out-of-the-money options are cheaper than at-the-money options, so the cost will be less.

> Sellers rely on the market staying flat or relatively neutral. The buyers typically are expecting a large price move.

The other negative for buyers of uncovered straddles or strangles is time decay. As the options move towards expiry, the holder will lose an increasing amount of the premium due to time decay (see figures). If the market turns out to be as volatile as the buyer expected, the time decay loss could be recouped (in whole or part); otherwise the buyer loses on two sets of premiums. Roth's advice for buyers of uncovered strangles is to get rid of the losing side early.

Gary Pickholz, portfolio manager at Yield Enhancement Strategists, said he looks at the strategies from a fixed-income perspective. Inherent in the pricing of options is the chance of instant, significant movement in price, Pickholz said. But even if the market makes a significant move in one day, it may not have exceeded the implied volatility band in the option's pricing. For instance, Pickholz said, the market might move 18/32 in one day. A volatility of 12/32 per day might be priced into the options. Provided that the options did not continue to move at more than an average rate of 12/32 per day through the life of the options, the volatility assumption should be valid. If the market priced the options based on the significant move, this could provide an opportunity to sell volatility, Pickholz said. On the other hand, a buying opportunity might arise when the market prices volatility from the close of one day's business to the close of the next, ignoring the tremendous volatility that can take place between closes, he said.

BULLS, BEARS, BUTTERFLIES AND BACKS

Option spreads provide several strategies that investors typically use as more conservative or less expensive alternatives to buying or selling individual options. Spreads can enable buyers to pay less for their options or they can help sellers reap premium gains without unlimited risk. In addition, by buying one option and selling another with the same expiry—one spread strategy—the investor can escape the worst ravages of time decay and is then free to pursue a longer-term strategy.

Susan Webb, v.p. and head of equity derivatives at Banque Paribas in New York, divides spread plays into three categories: vertical spreads, horizontal spreads and diagonal spreads. Vertical spreads, which Webb describes as those most commonly used, are manufactured by buying an option and selling an option with different strikes, but the same expiration. Horizontal spreads are put together with the same strike but different expirations, and diagonal spreads involve different strikes and different expirations.

Spreads can also be broken up into bull and bear spreads and credit or debit spreads, Webb explains. Bull spreads are bets on the underlying appreciating and bear spreads are bets on the underlying depreciating. An investor receives premium on a credit spread and pays premium on a debit spread. Webb says that, as a rule of thumb, bull spreads constructed from puts are credit spreads, whereas bear spreads created with puts are debit spreads. Conversely, a player would receive premium from a bear spread constructed from calls and pay for a bull call spread. (This rule may not hold true for diagonal spreads, however.)

Bull spreads can be created using puts or calls. For example, a bull spread, where the underlying was at 50, could be created by selling 55 strike calls and buying 50 strike calls. This would be a debit spread, explains Brett Kellam, sr. v.p. at Lehman Brothers. The cost of the at-the-money call purchase would only be partially offset by the sale of the out-of-the-money calls, because at-the-money calls usually would be more expensive than the out-of-the-money contracts. The call sale would place a cap on the gains that the strategy could reap, but the play is still bullish because it relies on the price of the underlying increasing more than the net premium that the investor has paid.

Bull and bear, credit and debit spreads can also be created using puts. A bull, credit spread constructed with puts might involve sell-

BACK SPREAD

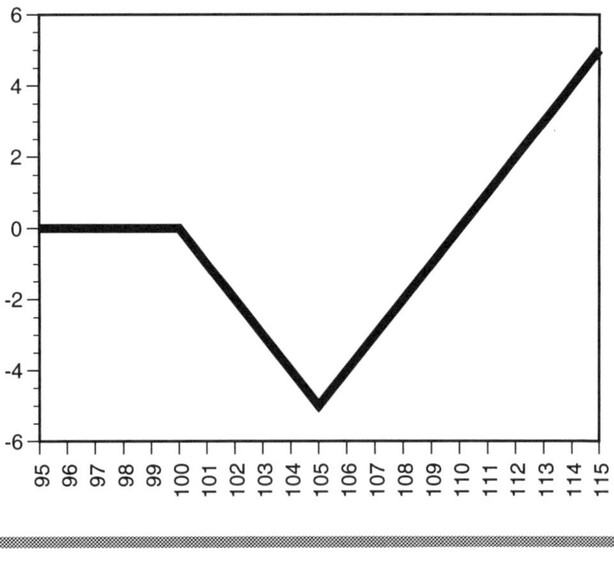

ing a 50 strike at the money put and buying a 45 strike out-of-the-money put. The investor wins if the options expire with the underlying trading above 50. The pickup from the trade comes from the high premium on the at-the-money put and the protection from the downside (which would otherwise be unlimited) comes from the purchase of the 45 strike put.

> Bull spreads can be created using puts or calls.

Butterfly spreads could be constructed in the same scenario (with the price of the underlying still at 50) by buying a 45 call, selling two 50 calls and buying one 55 call. Steve Temes, sr. v.p. at Oppenheimer & Co., explains that butterfly spreads are a way to take advantage of volatility. By selling two options at strikes where the volatility premium is highest, it is possible to create a relatively cheap strategy. In addition, says Temes, butterflies can benefit from time decay: as premiums erode, the two calls sold in the middle will lose extrinsic—implied volatility—value and move closer to the price of the underlying.

With this type of spread, the investor would make the most money if the options expire with the underlying trading near the middle of the range. As long as the underlying trades there, the calls the spread player has written are paying out nothing or very little and the call bought at the bottom end is deep in-the-money. If the underlying appreciates much more, the butterfly buyer will find himself paying out on two options.

Another of the family of spread trades is a back spread. This would involve selling one at-the-money call and buying two out-of-the-money calls. The general idea is to buy premium cheap. If, for instance, the at-the-money call had a strike of 100 and the out-of-the-money calls had strikes of 105, the spread player might not make money until the underlying was at 110, because of the extra premium paid. But past that point the spread provides the equivalent of a free call.

BARRIER OPTIONS

Barrier options—knock-ins and knock-outs—are contracts that are triggered or, more commonly, extinguished when the underlying asset price surpasses a given level. For example, a knock-out put on the dollar/Deutsche mark exchange rate would expire worthless if the dollar strengthened beyond a certain point. Because of the chance that they might be extinguished before expiration, barrier options tend to be cheaper than vanilla options, according to Robert Benson, head of equity derivatives at Midland Montagu in London.

Conceptually, the buyer of a knock-out option might be viewed as buying an option and selling a call on that option to the writer, explained Mark Ferron, v.p. in financial engineering and risk management at Bank of America in San Francisco. The writer's call would become exercisable when the underlying asset price surpasses the barrier, allowing the writer to repossess the knock-out option.

While in theory investors can trade barrier options based on any underlying asset, they are most common in the currency markets. Benson says the options are used mostly for speculation. Traders who have a strong view on the direction of a currency, and who are therefore confident that the currency will not reach a given barrier, might buy a knock-out option and save money. Alternatively, the trader might write a knock-out option, betting that the underlying will move strongly out of the money so that the option is extinguished early.

Knock-outs can also be useful to the hedger. Benson offered the example of a corporation buying a knock-out option to hedge some foreign currency exposure. If the exchange rate moves out of the money and hits the barrier, the option would be extinguished and the corporation would hedge itself with a forward contract, Benson said. The forward would lock in the corporation's gain on the underlying foreign exchange exposure, protecting it against future loss but at the same time closing off the possibility of further gains.

On the interest rate side, a corporation might buy a knock-out cap, Ferron said. The knock-out cap, which would be cheaper than an ordinary cap, would protect the corporation against an increase in short-term interest rates, but it would disappear if rates fell beneath the barrier. This instrument would be especially popular when the yield curve is steep, and corporate treasurers believe short-term rates are unlikely to fall.

Further hedging possibilities present themselves when the option's barrier and the exercise price are based on two different underlying assets or indices. Kosrow Dehnad, v.p. for product development and structuring at Chase Securities in New York, said that a mining company, for example, might sell a Prime cap with a barrier linked to the price of gold. As a result, the mining compa-

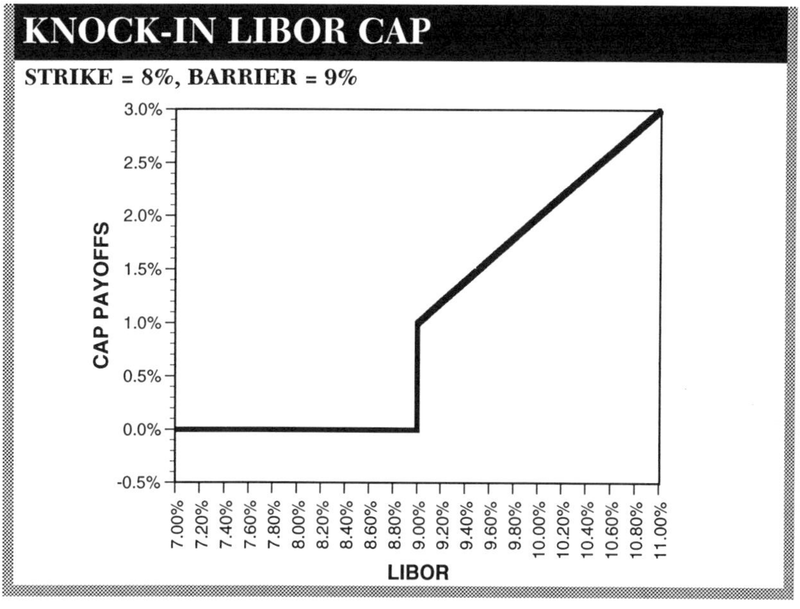

ny's short Prime cap would conveniently disappear when the price of gold fell, which is also when the company would be in a less favorable financial position. Similarly, a trucking company that has exposure to the price of oil might sell an interest rate floor that is triggered only when the price of oil falls below a barrier. The result is that the trucker has to pay out on the floor only when its own fuel costs are lower and the company is in a better financial position.

> Traders who have a strong view on the direction of a currency, and who are therefore confident that the currency will not reach a given barrier, might buy a knock-out option...

No matter what the user's strategy, the writer of a barrier option faces a difficult hedging problem. A knock-out option loses value very quickly as the underlying passes through the barrier. On the other hand, a knock-in option gains value as the underlying surpasses the barrier. In either case, the barrier option's delta—the rate of change of the option's price relative to the price of the underlying asset—jumps straight up when the barrier is penetrated. An option trader who is short a knock-out option might try to delta hedge: as the underlying price changes, he would buy or sell increasing amounts of the underlying to keep up with the changing value of the option. But when the option is extinguished as the underlying moves through the barrier, the trader may find it difficult to unwind his hedge quickly enough when the option's delta plummets, Benson said.

Dehnad said that one way to handle the problem of discontinuity in delta and gamma is to price the barrier option as if its delta changed continuously. Such an option would be slightly more expensive than a pure barrier option, and the extra premium would help compensate the dealer for the greater difficulty in hedging his exposure. Lester Wigler, president of the derivatives consulting firm The Credo Group in Stamford, Conn., suggested that a dealer might simply buy a collar as a hedge against a short knock-out put. Buying a standard put with the same strike as the knock-out put would be too expensive, since barrier options tend to be cheaper than standard options. But by selling an out-of-the-money call, the dealer would reduce the cost of his hedge.

LOOKBACKS AND LADDERS

Lookback options allow users to buy an underlying asset at its lowest price over a period of time, or to sell the asset at its highest price, according to Satish Nandapurkar, head of new products and exotic options at Swiss Bank Corp. in Chicago. A lookback call, therefore, allows traders to use 20-20 hindsight by buying an at-the-money call when the underlying asset is at its low for a period; owning a lookback put is equivalent to buying an at-the-money put at the high. "You never miss the best price," says Edmond Levy, chief foreign currency options trader at Barclays Bank in London.

The ability to act with the benefit of hindsight does not come free. After all, lookbacks always finish in-the-money, or at least at-the-money, if the low point for the underlying is also the closing price for the period. Christopher Bourdain, manager of foreign exchange sales at Crédit Suisse in New York, says that lookbacks generally cost much more than standard options.

Even if the lookback finishes in-the-money, the user may not have made money on the trade. Volatility in the underlying market will have to be high if the user's profit is to outweigh the hefty premium paid for the lookback. "If realized volatilities are very high, you're going to make out very well," says Joe Brennan, managing director at Sumitomo Bank Capital Markets in New York. The user who "envisions short, sharp moves" may benefit from lookback options, says Bourdain. If he expects gradual moves, however, the user might do better to pay the much lower premium on standard options.

A trader who believes volatility will remain low might sell a lookback and pocket the extra premium. Lookback sellers can hedge their short position by using straddles, says Levy. If the trader sells a lookback call, he would buy an at-the-money put and an at-the-money call. Each time the underlying asset hits a new low, the trader sells the old straddle and buys a new one. The profit on the old put, which will be in-the-money when the underlying hits a new low, helps to fund the purchase of new at-the-money calls and puts. In this way, the trader is guaranteed to have purchased an at-the-money call at the underlying asset's lowest price for the period, and the last call he buys will finish in-the-money by the same amount as the lookback call. In practice, however, the bid-offer spreads on the straddles and the timing of the rebalancing may reduce the efficiency of the hedge.

Similar to the lookback option is the lookforward. This option gives the buyer the difference between the underlying asset price at the beginning of the period and its high or low over that period, says Jacques Pezier, director at Mitsubishi Finance International in

PAYOFFS ON A LOOKBACK CALL AND A LOOK FORWARD CALL

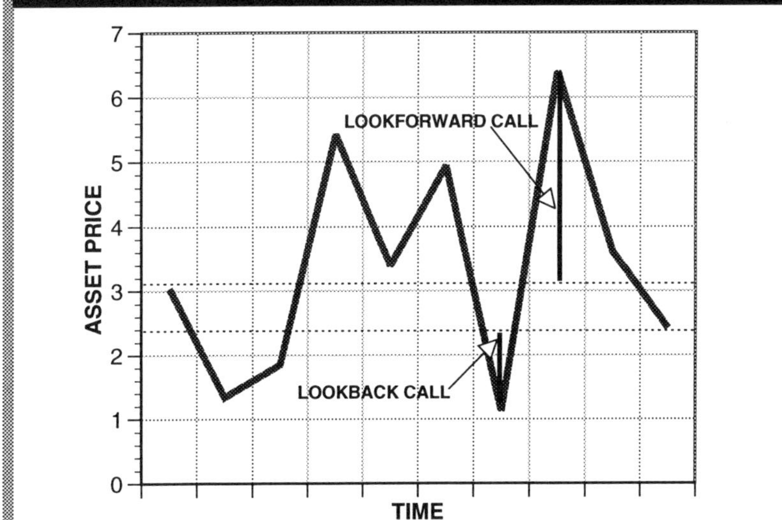

London. Owning the underlying asset and buying a lookback put—buying the asset and selling it at its high for the period—is equivalent to owning a lookforward call.

> Lookback options allow users to buy an underlying asset at its lowest price over a period of time, or sell the asset at its highest price.

One way to save on the premium expense of lookbacks and lookforwards is to buy a ladder option. A ladder call option guarantees the buyer that he will receive the difference between the strike and the highest of a series of threshold prices crossed by the underlying asset, or the expiration price, whichever is higher. For example, a ladder call linked to a stock index, the most common type of ladder option, might have an at-the-money strike and thresholds, or rungs, at 33%, 67% and 100% above the strike. If the index rises to 70%, for example, during the life of the option and then falls back, an investor owning such a call could be sure of receiving a return of 67% because the index rose above that rung. An investor who must hold an asset for some minimum number of years to secure tax advantages might find a ladder structure attractive, according to Nandapurkar.

The price of a ladder option depends on how many rungs it has and how far the rungs are from the strike, Nandapurkar says. Some ladders are capped, and are typically cheaper than uncapped options, since the investor is essentially selling an out-of-the-money call to offset some of his premium expense, he adds. If the rungs are placed close enough together, the ladder begins to resemble a lookforward option, Pezier says.

EXCHANGES FOR PHYSICALS

An exchange for physicals (EFP), also known as an "against actual" (AA), is an exchange of futures for the cash commodity or vice versa, according to James McConnon, sr. v.p. and chief investment officer at RXR Capital Management in Stamford, Conn. The transaction may occur during or after exchange trading hours, and open interest may be created or destroyed, depending on exchange regulations. Usually, however, a trader must be a commercial user of the commodity or financial asset (or at least a large speculator with access to the cash market) in order to engage in EFPs.

EFPs had their roots in agricultural trading, says Fred Grede, v.p. for administration and planning at the Chicago Board of Trade. EFPs first began when futures traders needed to make delivery of physical commodities at times or locations that did not conform to the CBOT's regulations. Grede estimates that EFPs account for 5% of the exchange's total volume. EFPs are probably used most widely in the gold, silver and currency markets, where active, 24-hour cash markets exist, according to John Hannam, chairman of Crédit Lyonnais Rouse USA in New York. EFP activity is heating up in the energy sector, driven by a growing OTC market, McConnon said.

U.S. regulators require that the physical asset exchanged bear some resemblance to the asset underlying the futures contract, but it need not be identical. With the Finex's Dollar Index futures, for example, a trader can exchange a customized basket of currencies for the futures, rather than a basket exactly mirroring the index, according to Richard Jaycobs, managing director at the Finex. As a result, the net position of a trader executing an EFP may not change, but his basis will, Jaycobs points out.

Exchanges vary in the degree to which they accommodate EFPs. Finex, within certain limits, allows them 24 hours per day. The New York Mercantile Exchange, on the other hand, restricts EFPs to normal trading hours, and LIFFE forbids them altogether.

EFPs allow investors to trade out of positions when the futures exchange is closed. McConnon offers July 3, 1992 as an example. Sterling became more volatile that day, while the U.S. futures exchanges were closed for Independence Day, and banks in the U.S. and Europe were open. An investor who was long International Monetary Market sterling futures and wanted to get out of his position could do so with an EFP (see figure). First the investor would sell sterling in the interbank market. Then, in a single transaction with the same counterparty, he would buy sterling and sell IMM futures. The cash transactions are necessary so that the investor can exchange cash for futures, a prerequisite for EFPs. The two cash transactions net out, leaving the investor with no futures position. On Monday, the investor would notify his futures broker of the EFP, and the broker would announce the trade at the exchange.

STERLING FOR IMM FUTURES EFP

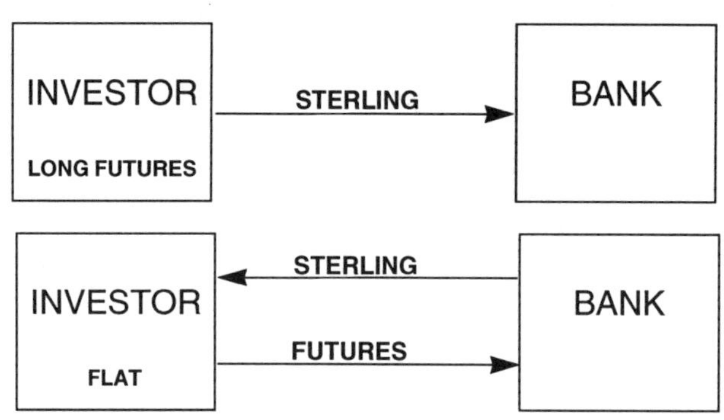

Finex has told swap dealers that they can EFP into the exchange's five-year Treasury auction futures, which are based on the when-issued five-year note. Ordinarily, two swap dealers entering into a fixed-for-floating swap would hedge the deal by exchanging Treasury notes: The fixed-rate payer would buy Treasury notes. As an alternative, the floating-rate payer could give five-year Treasury auction futures to the fixed-rate payer; in essence, the "physical" in the EFP is the fixed payer's payment stream.

In essence, an EFP is very similar to a basis trade, in which a trader sells futures and buys the underlying or vice versa.

In addition to facilitating transactions when the exchange is closed, EFPs can help investors save on transaction costs. EFPs are usually quoted in terms of a spread to the cash price. Unwinding a position with a single EFP is cheaper than doing two trades—and paying two bid-ask spreads. These savings sometimes make EFPs a more attractive way to trade between futures (or options combinations) and stocks in equity portfolios, according to Kevin Clark, v.p. for fixed income, indexing and hedging at UBS Asset Management (New York).

In essence, an EFP is very similar to a basis trade, in which a trader sells futures and buys the underlying or vice versa. A great deal of basis trading in the U.S. government bond market is done away from the CBOT, Grede says. The exchange's purchase of an electronic interdealer bond brokerage system from EJV Partners will give CBOT members better access to the cash bond market, Grede says, and should allow the exchange to recapture some of the basis trading business.

YIELD CURVE SWAPS

Yield curve swaps are agreements between two parties to exchange cash flows based on the difference between interest rates at two different points on a given yield curve. For example, an investor might agree to receive six-month LIBOR and to pay the yield on 10-year Treasuries minus a spread, with both payments to be reset every six months. These floating-for-floating swaps allow users to bet on the slope of the yield curve or to hedge the risk incurred in funding short and investing long.

Yield curve derivatives began as options on bonds of different maturities, according to Ian Hall, first v.p. at Republic National Bank of New York in London. As the interest rate derivatives market grew, however, swaps based on the dollar swaps yield curve became more popular. Now a typical yield curve swap might involve payments based on six-month LIBOR versus the seven-year swap rate, or the two-year swap rate versus the five-year swap rate, Hall says. Yield curve swaps, a type of basis swap, can mix and match payments based on a number of different reference rates, however. Strictly speaking, a LIBOR versus 10-year Treasury swap is really two trades in one: a floating-for-floating T-bill versus 10-year note swap and a basis swap between T-bills and LIBOR, notes Armand Tatevossian, director-financial products group at Barclays de Zoete Wedd in New York. Yield curve swaps are especially popular when there are widespread differences of opinion on the future shape of the yield curve.

One advantage of yield curve swaps is that they allow investors to take a view on the future shape of the yield curve without worrying about convexity or duration, Hall says. An investor who wants to bet on the flattening on the Treasury yield curve could sell, say, the two-year note and buy the 10-year note, but this trade can quickly become more complicated than it looks. Duration, a measure of the sensitivity of a bond's price to changes in interest rates, increases with maturity. Because the price of the 10-year note will change faster for a given change in interest rates than will the price of the two-year note, to avoid gaining or losing from parallel yield curve shifts the investor should short more of the two-year note that he buys of the 10-year. A bond's duration changes as its price changes, however, so to remain neutral on overall bond market moves, the investor must continuously rebalance his position. By entering into a yield curve swap, the investor shifts the burden of continuous rebalancing to the swaps dealer.

The fair value of a yield curve swap can be calculated by looking at the forward curves for the shorter and the longer maturity, Tatevossian says. If the spot yield curve is positively sloped, the present value of the projected long-end payments will outweigh

FORWARD 5-YEAR U.S. DOLLAR SWAP RATES VERSUS FORWARD 6-MONTH

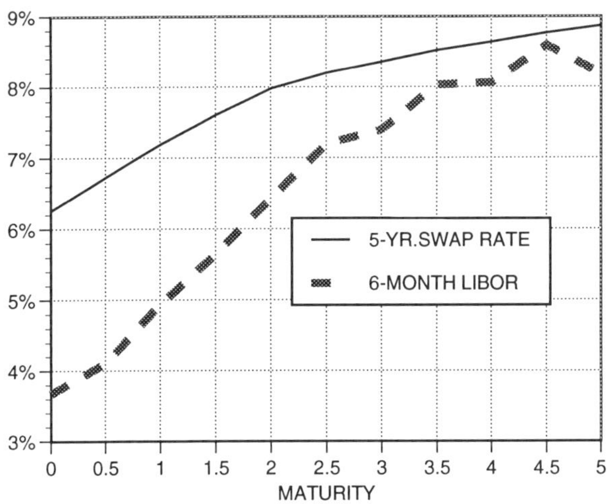

the projected short-end payments. To find the appropriate swap spread, the dealer will calculate the constant spread that will balance the present value of the two projected payment streams.

Investors can buy yield-curve options as well as swaps. Caps, floors and swaptions are available on yield curve swaps, Hall says. For example, a cancellable yield curve swap contains an embedded swaption, he says. Investors can even play the shapes of yield curves in different currencies by entering into cross-currency yield curve swaps, Hall adds. For example, investors can trade options on the spread between the 10-year Bund and the 30-year U.S. Treasury bond, Tatevossian says.

AVERAGE-RATE OPTIONS

Average-rate options, also called "Asian" options, are based on the average price of the underlying asset, rather than the spot price. When the strike is known in advance, average-rate options entitle the holder to the amount by which the average price over a set period is above (for a call) or below (for a put) the strike price.

The process of averaging the underlying asset price smooths out the volatility in the underlying, so average-rate options tend to be cheaper than standard options. "A great advantage of this kind of option is that highs and lows can cancel each other out," says Kosrow Dehnad, v.p. for product development at Chase Securities in New York.

The average on which an option is based can be calculated in different ways. How much the averaging process reduces volatility depends on how the average is taken, according to Gary Taratunio, v.p. at Chemical Bank in New York. A daily average will be much less susceptible to being moved by sudden changes in the spot price than will a monthly average.

For budgeting and forecasting purposes, corporate treasurers who regularly buy or sell a given commodity or currency are most concerned about its average price over a year. As a result, an average-rate option "offers them better protection from a budget point of view," says Renaud Vielfaure, head of currency options marketing at Société Générale in New York.

Sudden, isolated spikes in the price of the underlying have a smaller effect on an average rate option than they do on the more expensive standard options. A corporate treasurer primarily concerned with the average price, therefore, might be "over-insuring" by buying a standard option, Dehnad says. If the treasurer's exposure is heavier in part of the year, the average price can be weighted to reflect that, adds Edmond Levy, senior manager at Nomura Bank in London.

Average-rates are also useful for hedging thinly traded assets. The averaging process makes it harder to manipulate the underlying market. As a result, a six-month oil option might be settled against the average price on the last five trading days of the contract's tenor, says Levy.

On the interest-rate side, average-rate options are available as caps or floors on average LIBOR, says Vielfaure. Investors can even buy long-term options on equity indexes, he says.

The strike price of an average-rate option may not be known in advance, according to Taratunio. In that case, the strike is set to the average price of the underlying at expiration, and the value of the option is equal to the amount by which the final spot price is above (for a call) or below (for a put) the average.

Average-rates, like barrier options or lookbacks, are "path-

AVERAGE RATE CALL OPTION

STRIKE = 20 AVERAGE = 25.79 PAYOFF = 5.79

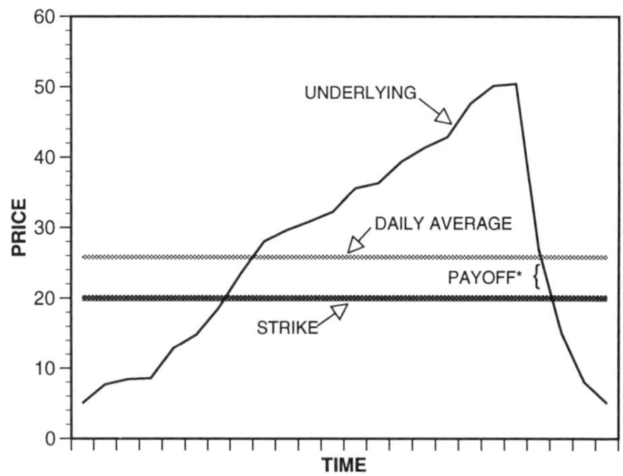

dependent" options. At expiration, the value of a standard options depends on the difference between the strike and the price of the underlying. A path-dependent option's value at expiration is influenced by how the underlying asset price moves during the option's lifetime. In fact, a massive one-day move in an asset price close to expiration could render a standard option worthless, while an average-rate option might stay in the money (see figure).

> A corporate treasurer primarily concerned with the average price, therefore, might be "overinsuring" by buying a standard option...

Because average-rates are path-dependent, traders try to estimate their value using Monte Carlo simulations, Dehnad says. In a technique similar to that used in the mortgage-backed securities market, traders make certain assumptions about volatility and forward rates, determine the value of the option for each of a large number of random paths, and take an average of the values for all the paths. The problem, says Dehnad, is that the process can be error-prone unless a large number of paths are used, and that may be too time-consuming. As a result, analysts have developed a number of computational techniques to improve the accuracy of the simulations, he adds.

The sensitivity of an average-rate option's price to changes in the underlying (delta) is much greater early in the life of the option than later, Dehnad points out. This is because the average is calculated based on a few prices, so that a big move in one price will move the average a great deal. As a result, for a given movement in the underlying asset price, a trader trying to delta-hedge a short position in average-rate options will have to adjust the hedge much more early in the options' lifetime than later. In essence, delta and gamma (the rate of change of delta with respect to the underlying) are "front-loaded" in average-rate options, Dehnad says.

COMPOUND OPTIONS

A compound option is simply an option to purchase another option, according to Alan Burnett, bond options trader at CS First Boston in London. The underlying option can be a call or a put. Hedgers can use compound options to protect an exposure that may or may not materialize, and speculators can use them to take a view on the volatility of the ultimate underlying asset. The compound option often has a much shorter tenor than the underlying option, Burnett adds.

Compound options are found in the currency and interest rate markets, and to some extent, in the equity market. A compound FX option might be useful to a corporation bidding for a contract in another currency, says David Durst, assistant v.p. of foreign exchange at Crédit Lyonnais in New York. The corporation will need to buy an FX option to hedge its exposure only if it wins the contract, and the contract will not be awarded for a month. The compound option would allow the corporation to buy an FX option and hedge itself if it wins the contract. As an alternative to buying a compound option, the corporation could simply buy a currency option and sell it later if it fails to win the contract, according to Durst. An 18-month call option, after all, will not lose all its value during the month it takes to find out the results of the bidding. The premium on the compound option, however, will be a fraction of that on the underlying option.

A corporation that may have to borrow money to fund a proposed project could use a compound option on interest rates to hedge that contingent exposure, according to Armand Tatevossian, director of the global swaps and options group at Barclays Bank in New York. Rather than waiting to find out if it will have to borrow the funds and then hedge by buying an interest rate cap—thereby exposing itself to both increases in the level of interest rates and in volatility—the corporation could buy an option on a cap, or a caption. (Options on floors are known as floortions.) Compound options are also traded on U.S. Treasury securities.

The total cost of hedging an exposure will be higher if the hedger pays a lower premium for the compound option and pays more to exercise into the underlying option, according to Durst. Suppose, for example, that a trader pays $1 for an at-the-money compound option on an underlying option with a premium of $10. If, when the compound option expires, the underlying option is trading at $15, the trader pays only the compound strike price of $10 to exercise into the underlying option, giving a total premium of $11 for the underlying option. If he pays $0.50 for an out-of-the-money compound option with a strike of $15 and the underlying option finishes at $15, then he must pay $15 to exercise (or $15.50

PRICES FOR COMPOUND CALL OPTION AND UNDERLYING CALL OPTION AS A FUNCTION OF STOCK PRICE

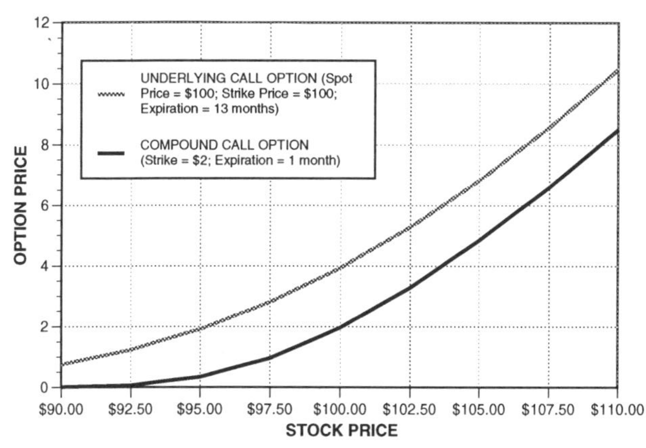

including the $0.50 compound option premium).

The value of a compound option depends on the value of the underlying option, which is in turn driven by the volatility of the ultimate underlying asset. As a result, compound options provide speculators with a way to bet on increases in volatility by risking a relatively small amount of money. Mark Malcomson, director of the Sunrise Company in London, says compound equity options have been used in this manner. On the other hand, speculators can use compound puts (the right to sell an option at a given price), which are rare, to bet against volatility, says Burnett.

A compound FX option might be useful to a corporation bidding for a contract in another currency...

Captions might provide a good way to express a view on the shape and volatility of the interest-rate swap curve, says Tatevossian. A steep U.S. dollar LIBOR curve implies that short-term rates are expected to rise quickly in the future, so a cap buyer would pay for a lot of forward intrinsic value. A corporate hedger who believes that the yield curve will flatten and volatility will decrease would expect to pay less if he buys a cap in the future; the purchase today of a caption would protect his future cash outlay for the cap should the opposite scenario occur.

The delta (the change in an option price with respect to a change in the underlying) of a compound option will be lower than the delta of the underlying option when the compound option is out of the money, Durst says. As the underlying option appreciates, however, and it becomes more likely that the compound option will be exercised, its delta will approach that of the underlying option, he adds (see figure). Indeed, a deep-in-the-money compound option begins to look like a forward on an option, Tatevossian notes.

MUNICIPAL SWAPS

Municipal interest rate swaps are not unlike plain vanilla interest rate swaps in which counterparties exchange floating for fixed rate payments. But unlike interest rate swaps executed by corporations, where managing interest rate exposure and lowering borrowing costs are paramount, "Tax is what drives this market," says Peter Shapiro, sr. v.p. at EuroBrokers in New York.

Certain states have high income-tax levels and issue bonds with double- or triple-exempt interest income, making these and other in-state municipal bonds very attractive to resident wealthy investors. Shapiro says there are 11 states—including California, New York, New Jersey and Connecticut—in which municipal securities are so popular among wealthy investors that mutual fund companies have established special tax-exempt money market funds to cater to them.

This demand for municipal bonds allows municipalities to take advantage of an arbitrage, typically at the efficient short end of the municipal curve. Although they desire fixed-rate debt because they receive primarily fixed revenues, from taxes, tolls and other fees, municipalities are able to issue floating-rate debt at lower levels than fixed. By issuing floating-rate debt and swapping for fixed—usually pegged to the benchmark J.J. Kenny or Public Securities Association indices—municipalities can structure their debt at the lowest cost to taxpayers. Even after paying annual remarketing and liquidity facility fees associated with issuing floating-rate debt, the municipalities come out ahead.

Private purpose bonds, typically issued for a specific private corporation or project, can take advantage of a similar arbitrage because they are subject to the alternative minimum tax (AMT). Particularly in states which do not have high-income tax rates, AMT issues are subject to a higher rate of taxation for certain wealthy investors. The bonds must therefore offer a higher interest rate and trade cheap to the market. The interest rate "penalty" is often greater in floating-rate paper than in fixed, says Shapiro. If an AMT issuer wants to issue floating-rate paper, it will be more advantageous for the issuer to issue fixed and swap into floating, he explains.

An important factor in structuring a municipal swap is ensuring that the municipality does not make a profit on the arbitrage, muni swaps professionals say. The U.S. federal government prohibits such profit-taking, primarily to prevent arbitraging between tax-exempt and taxable rates, and any profits garnered by municipalities must be forfeited to the government.

In order to prevent such arbitrage profits, municipalities often

MUNICIPAL SWAP CURVE

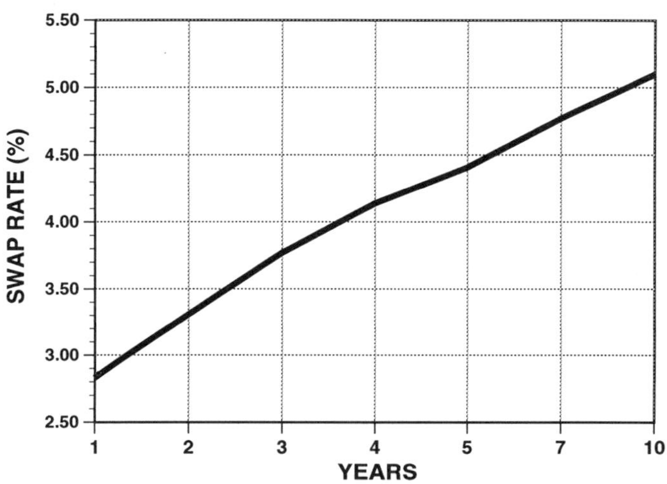

Mid-market figures(1992) for J.J. Kenny-based swaps for semi-annual settlement.

Source: ***Citicorp Securities Markets Municipal Finance***

enter into zero basis risk (or perfect) swaps. In such swaps, the maturity of the swap matches the maturity of the bond and the floating rate paid to the issuer matches the floating rate the issuer pays to the bondholders. So rather than paying a floating-rate relative to an index, the municipal swap counterparty pays a rate which matches the remarketing rate of the bond issue. But because the counterparty has to take on more risk by relying on the rates reset by the remarketing agent, it will typically offer less favorable swap terms.

The municipal swaps market has grown dramatically in the past few years as municipal debt has grown and local governments have become more comfortable with derivatives instruments.

The perfect swap also offers a practical advantage to the bond issuer. Municipalities and other revenue bond authorities issuing debt for projects such as roads or bridges operate in a "closed system" in which income is generated by tolls and other fixed sources. "It makes them averse to taking any kind of basis risk," explains one participant. The perfect swap gives them a fixed borrowing cost.

The municipal swaps market has grown dramatically in the past few years as municipal debt has grown and local governments have become more comfortable with derivatives instruments. Officials estimate that there are roughly 50,000 municipalities in the U.S., 8,000 of which come to market with debt annually. And not only has the market itself grown, but the swaps share of that market has increased as well.

Shapiro says the market is full of inefficiencies, but one of the most difficult aspects of the municipal market is educating the clientele. "They're not in the capital markets all the time," explains one participant.

RATIO SPREADS

Used by market makers to sell puts and calls, ratio spreading generally involves buying one option at a lower strike price and selling more of another at a higher strike price, usually in the same month. If 10 calls are bought and 20 are sold, the ratio is 2:1. If 10 calls are bought and 12 are sold, the spread is 12:10, or 1.2:1. The higher the ratio, the more dangerous the strategy, says Harrison Roth, first v.p. and senior options strategist at Cowen & Co.

For example, if the underlying of XYZ Inc. is at $85, a high ratio spread would be effected by buying 10 October $85 calls at $5.50 and selling 20 October $90 calls at $2.75. In selling twice as many options as were bought, no money would be invested, Roth explains. And if XYZ closes at $90 upon expiry, the short calls would not be exercised. Meanwhile, the long calls are worth $5.00 each and a tidy profit is realized. Although no money was invested, extra collateral was necessary to cover the short position, Roth explains. And if the stock goes over 90, the market maker has unlimited downside (see figure). The high 2:1 ratio can be very dangerous.

While lower ratios are less dangerous, Roth points out that the risk is still inherent. As soon as more options are sold than bought, the investor is in a short position with no theoretical downside limit.

Ratio spreads can be implemented for both equity and index options by using both calls and puts. The strategy is most popular among market makers who use it to maintain their own positions as part of their market making activities, according to Michael Schwartz, sr. v.p. and chief options strategist at Oppenheimer & Co. Market makers use combinations of ratio spreads, as well as butterflies and backs, to make markets in individual options. Because they have less stringent collateral requirements than retail investors, market makers can more readily implement the strategy. The market maker must constantly monitor the spread, as well. If the underlying increases in value the options may have to be rolled up, and if it decreases, the short option may have to be bought back.

Market makers use ratio spreads to remain delta neutral, says Roth. If someone wanted to buy calls from a market maker, the market maker would look at the deltas to devise his ratio spread strategy. If he saw two options with deltas of 50 and 70, he might buy five delta 70 calls and sell seven delta 50 calls. If the underlying increases in value by four points, the long calls will increase 70%, or 2.8 points, and the short calls will go up 50%, or 2.0 points.

The market maker will lose 14 points on the short position but gain an equal amount on the long position. The same thing would happen if the underlying decreased in value. "He'll be even in his ratio spread because he's weighted to the reciprocal of the two

TWO-TO-ONE RATIO SPREAD PAYOFFS

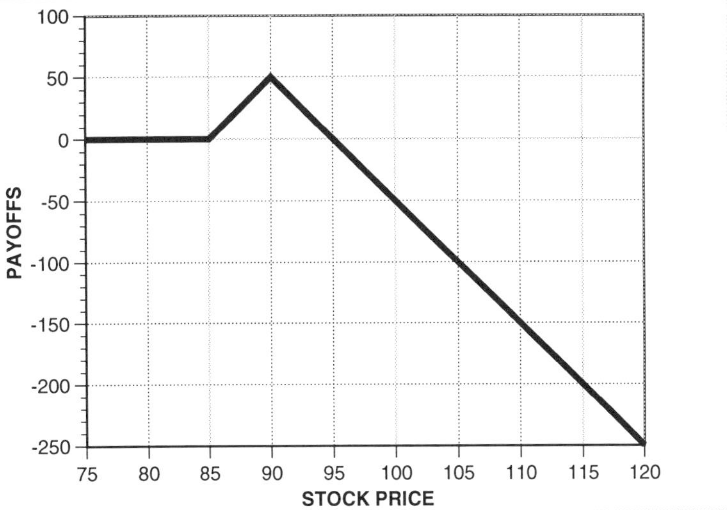

delta ratios," explains Roth. This is generally how market makers sell calls and puts.

The break-even point of a ratio spread can be determined by dividing the sum of the spread difference and the net credit of the position by the number of uncovered calls and adding the resulting quotient to the upper strike price, says Roth.

> "The risk to the retail investor is that he's got naked options out there...It's not for the faint of heart."

To use the XYZ Inc. example, if one October 85 call is bought for 5.5 and three October 90 calls are sold for 2.75, the net credit would be 2.75. The sum of the net credit and the spread difference would be 7.75. After dividing 7.75 by the two uncovered calls (3 7/8) and adding that quotient to the upper strike (90), we discover that if the underlying rises to 93 7/8, the market maker will break even. If it rises above 93 7/8, the position will be a money loser, according to Roth.

"The risk to the retail investor is that he's got naked options out there," explains Schwartz, noting that retail investors are more comfortable with covered spreads with equal numbers of puts and calls. "It's not for the faint of heart."

QUANTO OPTIONS

A quanto option is one of the family of currency-protected equity options. Quantos are also known as percentage change options, or currency-protected size options. They are often used when the local currency of the investor is different from the currency of the underlying asset in which he would like to invest. For example, quanto options are used to include currency protection for a dollar-based investor buying options on French franc equities, according to Donald Martocchio, principal and New York product manager for the synthetic equity group at Morgan Stanley.

The quanto option is designed to eradicate exchange rate risk associated with foreign equity investment. The quanto option achieves this goal by predetermining the exchange rate at which the intrinsic value of the option can be exchanged when it's exercised. For example, a U.K. investor may believe that the S&P 500 will perform well, but is worried that the dollar could weaken, thus hurting his sterling return, in which case a quanto option would be a viable alternative (see example).

Other variations of options could produce greater returns than a quanto. A reverse currency exchange option, for example, allows the investor to take advantage of the depreciation of the dollar outlined in the last example, but the reverse currency option also incorporates currency risk that is eliminated by the quanto option. The quanto is more widely used by investors who have a view on the equity market but have no view on the currency, or who simply do not want to take a risk on the fluctuation of the currency exchange rate, according to Martocchio.

Often, pension funds which invest in foreign equity markets use currency hedges to cover their exposure. Any rise in the underlying without any change in the exchange rate forces the pension fund to adjust its currency hedge to its equity value. According to Martocchio, the quanto has advantages over this strategy. "You could view the quanto as a flexible currency hedge. As the equity market moves, the size of your currency hedge is adjusted accordingly," he says.

The quanto should not be characterized as a currency option because it will not become in- or out-of-the-money on the exchange rate, explains Jacques Pezier, director at Mitsubishi Finance International. He classes a quanto as a split currency protection.

The Black-Scholes model can be used to price a quanto by mod-

ORDINARY VS. QUIANTO OPTION PAYOFFS

The payoff on an ordinary option in a domestic currency, with a strike at K and expiring at maturity T, when the underlying is in a foreign currency, where S_t is the underlying asset price at time maturity, and X_t is the value of one unit of foreign currency in domestic currency at maturity:

$$X_t \text{ Max}(S_t\text{-}K,0)$$

The payoff on a quanto option in a domestic currency, where X_0 is a fixed exchange rate in effect at the outset of the option:

$$X_0 \text{ Max}(S_t\text{-}K,0)$$

If a U.K. investor purchases a one-year call on the S&P 500 at a strike of 420, and the size of the option is $1 per S&P 500 point, with an exchange rate of 52p to the dollar, and at expiry the S&P 500 has moved up to 440, but the dollar has depreciated to 48p, the ordinary option would give a pay-off of:

0.48(440-420)= £9.60

A quanto, on the other hand, would give the following pay-off:

0.52(440-420)= £10.40

ifying certain inputs, according to Pezier. The discount factor is the domestic interest rate of the investor. The drift term is dependent upon the difference between the foreign interest rate, the dividend and the co-variance between the exchange rate and the underlying asset. The drift term represents the cost of carry related to the underlying asset for the term of the option. The volatility is the same as that of the underlying.

> "You could view the quanto as a flexible currency hedge. As the equity market moves, the size of your currency hedge is adjusted accordingly."

A quanto can be used on any underlying asset in a foreign currency, other than the currency itself, says Pezier. The quanto can also be combined with other options, according to Martocchio. Typical examples include use with outperformance options, spreads, and barrier options. The combination chosen depends upon an investor's specific trading view, says Martocchio.

"Even though there are some simple formulas for pricing exotic options such as quantos, the simple formula should be thought of as an approximation within a general risk management framework," says George Pastrana, principal and director of global equity derivatives research at Morgan Stanley. For example, longer-dated quanto options—as well as all long-dated options—are more sensitive to the movements in interest rates while short-dated options are affected more by a change in volatilities, Pastrana states. For quanto options in particular, the co-variance adjustment to the aforementioned drift term cannot be forecast with great precision and therefore can lead to wider bid/ask spreads than similar normal options of the same maturity, Pastrana notes.

INVERSE FLOATERS

Commonly used by issuers and investors who think that short-term rates will stay low or come down, inverse floaters are securities with coupon rates that rise as benchmark underlying interest rates fall, and vice versa. The coupon rate of an inverse floater is the predetermined strike rate minus the floating rate of interest (for example, LIBOR). An inverse floater is a combination of a swap, an issue and a cap, according to Kosrow Dehnad, v.p. in charge of new product development at Chase Securities.

If a company wanted to sell $100 million in debt and pay a spread over LIBOR, it would use the inverse floater to make the issue attractive to investors who expect LIBOR to remain static or fall. To create the inverse floater, the company enters into a swap paying LIBOR on $200 million to a bank, which in turn will pay fixed on $200 million to the issuer. The issuer can swap more than the value of the issue because when the cash flow is netted out it meets its funding target. The payment of fixed on $200 million can be defined as follows:

2 x fixed on $100 million

The final coupon rate the investor will receive when the spread over LIBOR on the debt instrument and the fixed payment are passed on to him by the issuer is:

2 x fixed on $100 million - LIBOR on $100 million

The issuer has been able to borrow at LIBOR on $100 million and the investor has a more attractive package. The inverse floater gives an investor the same benefits as if he were entering a swap himself. The larger the swap transaction, the greater the pickup rates for the investor if interest rates stay low, explains Dehnad.

Because steeply rising interest rates could theoretically cause the holder of the inverse floater to owe payments to the issuer, investors are always protected by a cap. The cap ensures a minimum coupon payment of zero. As the inverse floater is a mixture of swaps and caps on top of an issue, its price is made up of these individual components.

Inverse floaters do not necessarily need falling interest rates to produce big returns for investors, according to Phil Berent, v.p. in the investors strategies group at Merrill Lynch International. For example, consider a three-year Australian dollar inverse floater, where the predetermined strike rate is 22.06%, the floating rate is the bankers acceptance rate, and which pays coupons according to the following formula:

22.06 - (2 x 6 month BA rate)

With the BA rate at its current level of 5.79%, the coupon payment on the inverse floater will be 10.48%. According to Berent,

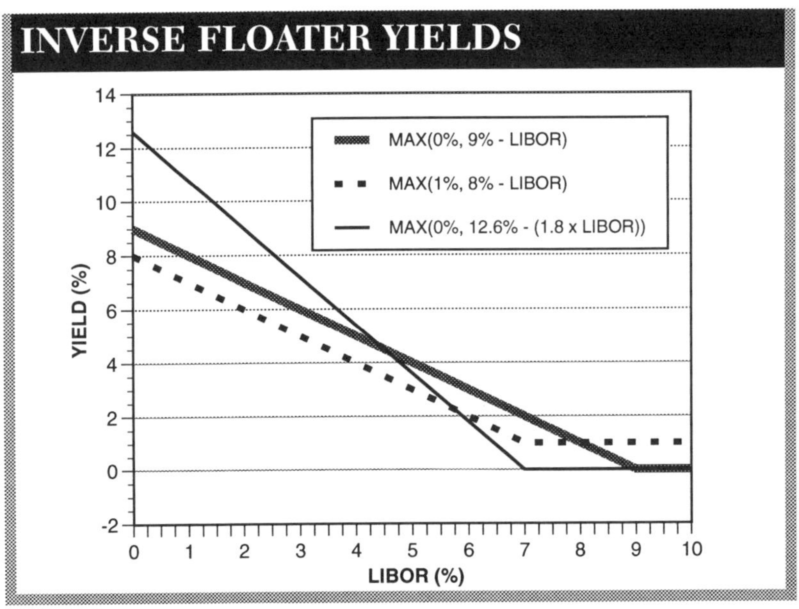

the returns on inverse floaters will only underperform compared to fixed or floating rate instruments of the same maturity if rates rise substantially.

The returns are greater when interest rates fall. The interest from an inverse floater would rise two ticks for every tick the BA rate falls. If the BA rate falls to 5.69%, then the coupon rate will rise to 10.68%. Conversely, the investor takes the risk that for every tick the BA rate increases, the inverse floater will lose two ticks.

> Inverse floaters do not necessarily need falling interest rates to produce big returns for investors.

For example, many investors recently were interested in buying inverse floaters in the European market in the belief that interest rates were going to fall, says Berent. But because the move was implied by the forward rates, coupon rates of such inverse floaters were low. To profit from a Deutsche mark-denominated inverse floater with a three-year maturity, yields would have had to fall 2.5% to outperform a fixed- or floating-rate Deutsche mark bond rate of similar maturity, Berent says. In contrast, the upward sloping yield curve in Australia meant that the inverse floater coupon rate was higher than the BA rate because investors were paid for taking a view against implied forward rates.

The price of an inverse floater is affected by the long-term interest rate (the interest rate of a standard instrument of the same maturity) and the coupon payment is affected by the short-term rate, says Berent. It is therefore a good way to achieve exposure to the long-term interest rate and, according to Berent, it gives a higher carry or coupon rate compared to an government bond if there is an upward yield curve.

In the U.S., some investors use inverse floaters to hedge mortgage-backed securities because in a falling interest rate environment mortgage prepayments rise. Inverse floaters are used to compensate for such an occurrence but the hedge is not clean, according to Dehnad. This is because of the lack of perfect correlation between medium- and long-term interest rates and short rates. Prepayments are most sensitive to medium- and long-term rates and a drop in those rates will not necessarily translate into a drop in short rates, says Dehnad. Banks and fund managers use them as alternative floating-rate instruments. Variations of inverse floaters include those that can be denominated in one currency and paid in another, necessitating the use of quanto options.

DIFF SWAPS

Differential (or diff) swaps enable counterparties to take advantage of global interest rate differentials without incurring currency exposures. In a diff swap, a counterparty pays a floating interest rate of one currency and receives a floating interest rate of another currency, plus or minus a spread, with payments denominated in a single currency, according to Bob Khanna, group head at Citibank's financial engineering department. Diff swaps are also known as switch, index, guaranteed exchange rate, quant or quanto swaps.

The main attraction of the vehicle is its hedge against currency exposure: counterparties make their payments "based on the same notional principal and denominated in the same currency," according to Khanna. The buyers of diff swaps are mostly money fund managers, corporate borrowers, securities firms and large banks which hope to reduce debt costs or pick up yield, according to Steve Gregornik, v.p. in charge of exotic swaps and options at Merrill Lynch International in London. The transaction allows investors to enhance yields by securing higher foreign interest rates and borrowers to cut interest payment costs by taking advantage of lower foreign interest rates.

A U.S. asset manager who must have his principal and coupon payments in U.S. dollars, for instance, might enter a U.S. dollar-denominated diff swap and receive DM LIBOR and pay U.S. LIBOR plus a spread. A U.S. corporate borrower, on the other hand, may want to reduce his cost of funding overseas by entering a DM-denominated diff swap. Such a swap, in which the borrower would receive DM LIBOR and pay U.S. dollar LIBOR plus a spread, would give the borrower a net foreign currency-denominated debt cost of U.S. dollar LIBOR plus a spread, says Khanna.

In both instances, the value of the structure is considerably enhanced if the swaps have tenors of three to five years because of the relative steepness of the U.S. dollar curve and the inversion/flatness of the European yield curves," adds Khanna. Tenors of up to 10 years are available and amounts up to $100 million are manageable in a single trade. Diff swaps can be composed of any currencies which have an active medium- to long-term swap market.

As for pricing, most lending institutions take a proprietary view, Gregornik said. "In a straightforward index swap where one counterparty receives DM LIBOR minus X on a U.S. notional amount and pays U.S. LIBOR flat on the same notional, you compare the implied forward interest rate differentials to solve for X, the spread."

Because market makers such as large banks and securities firms usually have trading books in several currencies they can "hedge a diff swap by the dynamic use of interest rate and foreign exchange positions" and thereby gain a pricing advantage, according to Khanna.

DIFF SWAP (settling in U.S. dollars)

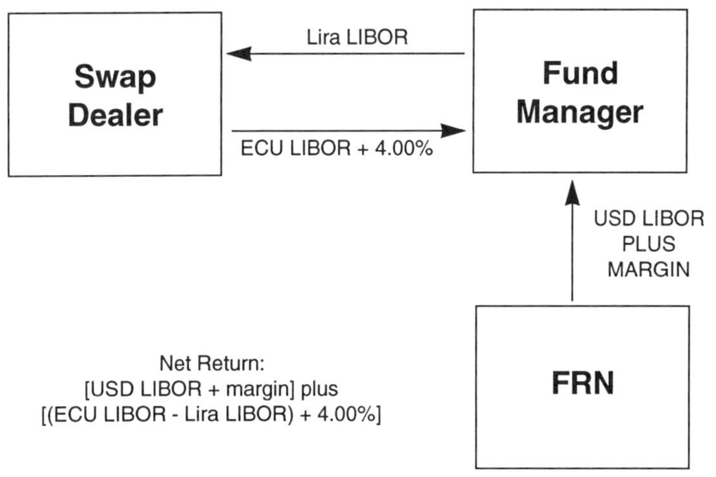

Source: ***Citibank***

COMMODITY SWAPS

A commodity swap is an agreement to exchange payments, typically fixed for floating, which are indexed to some market commodity price, according to William Winters, managing director and head of swaps at J.P. Morgan in London. Most commodity swaps involve oil and other energy-related products and, to a lesser extent, metals.

The fixed rate is determined by whatever price the seller thinks is an appropriate market rate at the time of the transaction. This rate remains set for the length of the swap, whether the swap covers one day (in which case the swap is called a "bullet swap"), one month, one year or the 10-year limit. Indeed, the flexibility that commodity swaps offer in terms of tenor is what constitutes their beauty, according to Teodor Kowalyk, associate-commodity derivatives at J.P. Morgan.

The floating rate is connected to an index, says Kowalyk. The most often used indices include the West Texas Intermediate (WTI)—or light sweet crude—futures contract traded on the New York Mercantile Exchange and the mean cash prices as quoted in Platts Oilgram Price Report for any crude oil around the world.

The players in the commodity swaps market include producers, consumers, investment houses and, more recently, institutional investors. Those most concerned about price fluctuations are producers, such as major domestic and foreign oil companies and independents, who produce oil for sale on the open market. "Producers are always motivated to be hedgers because they live and die with price variations with their commodity, and they always want to reduce price risk," says David Seaman, v.p.-currency and commodity products at Goldman Sachs & Co.

Consumers—including airlines, trucking companies, railroads, utilities and refiners—are traditionally more interested in protection against catastrophes and usually will not enter into a commodity swap but rather use a collar to protect themselves from large price movements, says Seaman.

The investment houses are large, established firms such as J.P. Morgan, Goldman Sachs and Bankers Trust who can either buy or sell commodities, while investors are mostly large institutions who want to invest in a commodity index because they are "negatively correlated with stocks and bonds," according to Seaman.

The commodity swap transaction itself is fairly straightforward. The oil producer, in this case the seller, decides for an agreed length of time to lock into the fixed price of $20 per barrel with an investment house (see illustration). Thus, in exchange for receiving a fixed price for the oil, the producer agrees to pay the investment house a floating rate, which is most often indexed to WTI because it's such a liquid market, or the more geographically specific Platts prices, according to Kowalyk.

WEST TEXAS INTERMEDIATE SWAP

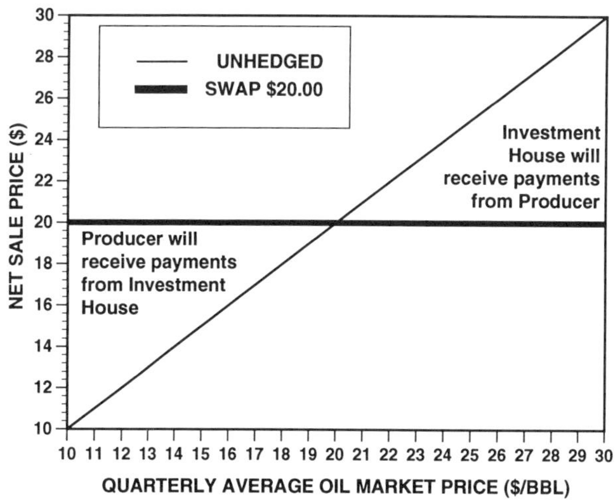

While the producer has the opportunity to do so, the investment house will most certainly hedge its commodity swap deal by conducting mirror transactions in the interbank market, much as it does with interest rates and currencies, according to Ron Neal, v.p. and head natural gas trader at Citibank. In addition, investment houses hedge their commodity swaps by lumping them together and thereby greatly reducing risk, according to Kowalyk.

> Consumers... usually will not enter into a commodity swap but rather use a collar to protect themsleves from large price movements.

Kowalyk also notes that the use of commodity swaps has been more prevalent in Western Europe than in the U.S. The turning point, he says, was the Gulf War. In an extreme example, some European airlines had locked in a July 1990 jet fuel price of $160-170 a metric ton using commodity swaps and options, says Kowalyk. When the price reached an October 1990 peak of $490 a metric ton, the Europeans were far more protected from the oil price runup than their American counterparts. "Only recently have American companies jumped on the learning curve when it comes to commodity hedging," says Kowalyk.

While the commodity swaps market is expanding rapidly, it comprises only a small percentage of the more than $3 trillion swaps market, says Neal.

FORWARD EXCHANGE AGREEMENTS

Counterparties in a forward exchange agreement (FXA) agree at the outset of the transaction to compensate each other for the differences which occur in the agreed foreign exchange swap margin between the dealing and settlement dates, using a notional outright forward rate as a basis of comparison, explained Robert Jasper, senior dealer-forward desk at Barclays Bank. The instrument, which evolved out of concerns about credit risk and capital constraints, is used mostly by banks taking a view on currencies or wanting to hedge their currency exposure.

Trevor Carr, foreign exchange and interest rate proprietary trader at Caisse Nationale de Crédit Agricole in London, said the FXA is to forward foreign exchange what the forward rate agreement is to the money markets. The FXA has the advantage over traditional hedging instruments such as cash forward exchange contracts in that no principal is exchanged and there is only one payment, made by the counterparty that is out of the money, he said.

If a trader has a particular view on likely interest rate differentials in six months, he may decide to purchase a 6 x 12 FXA, which will commence in six months, for a six-month contract period. On the fixing date, two days prior to the commencement of the contract, a comparison is made between the agreed outright rate and the spot settlement rate, and the agreed swap margin and the settlement swap margin.

In the accompanying example, the deal itself will not continue for the six months after the settlement date, rather the six-month contract period is taken into account in the swap margins set on the fixing date, according to Neil Fryer, director-deputy head of treasury at Charterhouse Bank. The deal itself comes off the books after the settlement date, he explained. This allows the investor to gain long-term risk exposure to forward exchange rates for a short tenor, according to Carr.

FXAs can be used to hedge FRAs and FX forwards, and vice versa, noted Jasper. FXAs can be priced in various ways, according to Fryer, by using the FRA market and the cash forward foreign exchange market. "It just depends on how you want to use it," he said.

An FXA is part of the family of synthetic agreements for forward exchange (SAFEs), according to Fryer. Its sister product is the exchange rate agreement (ERA) which differs from the FXA in

FXA SETTLEMENT AMOUNT

$$\left[A2 \times \left[\frac{(OER - SSR) + (CFS - SFS)}{1 + \frac{(L \times D)}{(100 \times B)}} \right] \right] - \left[(A1 \times (OER - SSR) \right]$$

Where:

A1 = First Contract Amount

A2 = Second Contract Amount

CFS = Contract Forward Spread

SFS = British Bank Association (BBA) Settlement Forward Spread

OER = Outright Exchange Rate

SSR = BBA Settlement Spot Rate

L = BBA Interest Settlement Rate for the Secondary Currency (expressed as a number and not as a percentage)

D = Number of calender days in the Swap Period

B = 360, or, if interest rates in respect of the Secondary Currency are calculated on a 365 day year basis, 365.

that it does not contain an outright forward rate, he explained. Both counterparties in an ERA agree only to compensate each other for differences in swap margins on the same basis as the FXA. This means the ERA counterparties are not exposed to adverse movements in spot rates, Fryer noted.

The forward exchange agreement is to forward foreign exchange what the forward rate agreement is to the money markets.

The SAFE products were created by Midland and Barclays six years ago, according to Fryer. The banks had grown aware of the question of capital adequacy and counterparty credit risk, which could cause liquidity problems in the forward markets. The products were not greeted with an immediate market demand but, over the last few years, the ERA and FXA markets have grown, according to Carr. Their increased popularity can be attributed to the fact that they reduce the capital requirements in hedging currency exposure and so smaller banks can especially benefit from the SAFE products, noted Jasper. Because FXAs are usually treated as interest rate products, there is a reduction in credit risk exposure for banks, he continued.

"There are about 20-25 banks that have traded FXAs across various currencies," said Fryer. U.K. banks have been at the forefront of the development of FXAs, as the U.S. forward foreign exchange market is less liquid than that of the U.K., according to Carr. But there is now more interest being shown in the SAFE products from New York, according to Jasper. Jasper also noted a growth in corporate interest in FXAs as a means of hedging currency exposure. The major currency deals in FXAs are against the dollar and include all the major currencies.

CONTINGENT PREMIUM OPTIONS

With the contingent premium option, "All you need is a dollar and a dream, and maybe you don't need the dollar," according to Emanuel Derman, v.p.-head of the Quantitative Strategies Group at Goldman Sachs & Co. The buyer of a contingent premium option pays a higher than usual premium for the option, but only if it finishes in the money, he says. The contingent option's premium is about double that of a plain vanilla option because the former has roughly a 50% probability of being exercised in the money, explains Armand Tatevossian, director of the global swaps and options group at Barclays Bank in New York. It is also known as a zero premium option because the buyer pays nothing for it initially.

Contingent premium options began in the commodity markets and became a popular vehicle for playing the Nikkei 225 before moving to the currency markets. End-users include corporations, asset managers and speculators. These options have been used as disaster insurance against currency devaluation within the Exchange Rate Mechanism, according to Tatevossian. Indeed, one reason to use the contingent premium option is that "you think the market is going very far down or up," according to Derman.

Contingent premium options belong in the category of limit-dependent options. That is, they are options with a trigger that either activates or renders inactivate the option based on an event or the level of an index, which can also be a function of an underlying asset, according to Kosrow Dehnad, v.p. in charge of new product development at Chase Securities in New York. Also in this category of options are barrier options and digital options. Barrier options (knock-ins and knock-outs) are triggered or extinguished when the underlying asset moves beyond a certain limit and are cheaper than regular options because they may be worthless before expiration. With digital options, the payouts are fixed and, like binary digital circuits that are either "on" or "off," digital options either pay the fixed amount or nothing at all.

A contingent option is actually two options: its buyer purchases a plain vanilla option from the dealer while concurrently selling back to the dealer a digital option, both of which have the same expiration and strike, explains Tatevossian. If the plain option expires in the money, the digital option's payoff at expiration is the predetermined price of the contingent premium option. Conversely, if the plain option expires out-of-the-money, the digital option's payoff is zero.

CONTINGENT PREMIUM OPTION PAYOFFS (as sum of two options)

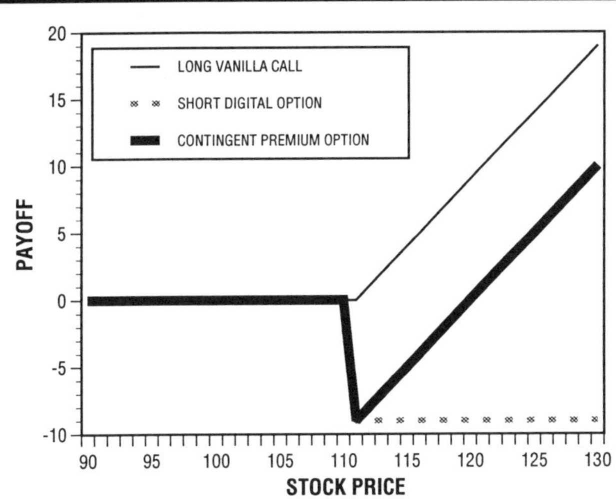

For instance, if an investor buys an IBM contingent premium call with a strike of 110 and a contingent premium of $9, and the call expires with the IBM stock at 110.01, then the call option is in-the-money and the buyer has to pay the $9 contingent premium back to the seller. Tatevossian notes that since the contingent premium option involves no payout of cash on the trade date, the sale of the digital option funds the purchase of the plain option. The fact that the two options essentially have the same value explains why a contingent premium option is also called a zero premium option, he says.

> With the contingent premium option, "All you need is a dollar and dream, and maybe you don't need the dollar."

As the contingent option approaches the strike price, the option's delta (the amount an option's price changes as the underlying moves one point in price) and its gamma (the amount the delta changes for every one point move in the underlying) can be very large. The large delta and gamma are reasons why investors must use contingent premium options carefully, as well as why they are used only with a view toward large price movements either up or down. Contingent options, says Derman, "look like a way to pay nothing, but there is an intermediate range where, if the call finishes in-the-money, you have to pay more than you received."

For example, suppose the investor purchases a zero premium call option on IBM for $9. If the call expires with IBM below 110, the buyer pays nothing, but if the option expires even slightly above 110—say to 110.01—the buyer would have to pay $9 while getting back only 0.01. Once the stock option hits the strike price, its payoff makes an abrupt vertical drop (see illustration). As the underlying moves beyond the strike price the payoff increases.

There are newer types of contingent premium options which are activated by an agreed upon trigger or event and are embedded in other derivative products such as swaps.

SYNTHETIC OPTIONS

Synthetic options seek to replicate standard options contracts at less expense by tracking an option's price relative to the underlying. Options traders and portfolio managers are the most common users of synthetic options, which they employ for hedging positions. Synthetic options offer a wide range of strategies, be they long or short positions, options on one underlying, an index or variety of currencies.

The key variable used to create many synthetic options is delta—the measurement of how much an option's premium will move in relation to the underlying price. The delta of the option being replicated is tracked to construct a synthetic option. Take for instance a U.S. portfolio manager who wants to hedge his foreign holdings and uses forwards to reproduce the effect of an at-the-money foreign currency put option with a delta of around 0.5. If the portfolio manager had $100 million worth of foreign underlying which he wanted to hedge back into dollars, he would sell forward $50 million, or 50% of the underlying. If the dollar were to weaken, then the option the portfolio manager would be tracking would move out of the money. The option's delta would therefore fall below 0.5, so the hedge would have to be reduced. This would be done by buying back forwards.

The use of forwards in the synthetic currency option means that no premium is paid at the beginning of the transaction as with an option. Instead the premium costs of the strategy are the losses incurred in buying back the forwards. The synthetic currency option can be less expensive than an OTC option. OTC options are priced in terms of implied volatility whereas forwards are priced in terms of spot and interest rate differentials. The spot and interest rate differentials are the basis of historical volatility and when compared, historical volatility has proven to be 0.5-1% below implied volatility. As the foreign exchange markets are very liquid, transaction costs are also low.

Synthetic option strategies can have limitations. The user is not locking into implied volatilities as he is with an option and there is the risk that realized volatility could be greater than implied volatility. The price action of the underlying can also have a significant impact on the cost of the synthetic strategy. If the market is characterized by a "whipsaw" effect (the price of the underlying rises up and down over the period), the cost of synthetic strategy will increase. Price savings on some synthetic options may not be that great. In a very liquid options market such as Treasury bonds, the bid-offer spreads are narrow anyway.

A synthetic option can contain an option as one of its elements. For instance, if an investor wanted to create a synthetic put he

SYNTHETIC VERSUS STANDARD OPTIONS ON FUTURES

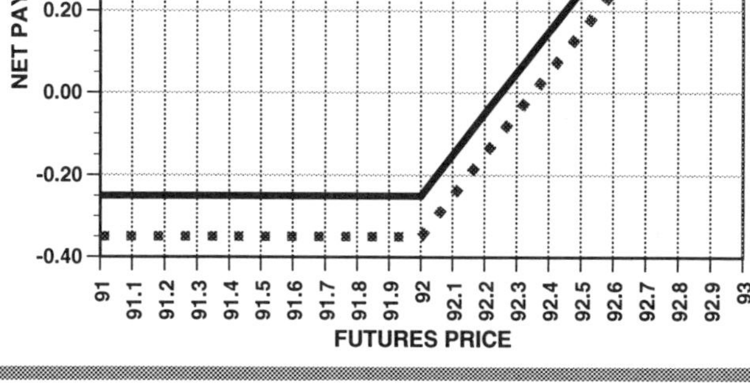

would buy a call and sell the underlying. Synthetic strategies containing options are also used for risk management and as a means of replicating a product at a cheaper price. For example, if a three-month interest rate future is trading at 91.80 and an investor wants to buy a 92.00 strike call which costs 35 basis points while a put of the same strike cost 45 basis points, a synthetic call can be created at a 10 basis point discount by buying both the put and the future. If in three months the future is at 92.50, the synthetic call holder gains 25 basis points (the 70 basis point gain on the future less the 45 basis point cost of the put) while the standard call holder gains only 15 basis points (the 50 basis point gain on the future less the 35 basis point cost of the call). Conversely, if in three months the future is at 91.50, the synthetic call holder loses only 25 (the 45 basis point cost of the put less the 20 basis point gain on the sale of the future), while the standard call holder loses the 35 basis point cost of the call (see box). In this example the position is not delta hedged.

Synethic options may become more prevalent as investors become more sophisticated and move away from traditional options.

The future of synthetic options with options in their structure is assured because they are used by options brokers who need to hedge their options books. Synthetic options may become more prevalent as investors become more sophisticated and move away from traditional options. The growth of the pension funds market should see a corresponding growth in dynamic currency products as the market for hedging products becomes larger.

RANGE FORWARDS

Range forwards involve simultaneously buying a call or put option and selling another of the opposite type (put or call), according to Armen Avanessians, v.p. in charge of currency and commodity strategies at Goldman Sachs in New York. The premium gained by the sale of one option offsets the premium paid for the other, so that the net premium paid is zero. If the user also has a position in the underlying, these contracts structurally create a range of rates within which the specified underlying will be exchanged at maturity. This range is created because the short call caps the upside gain on the underlying, while the long put limits the downside risk.

Yaron Zilberman, currently on leave from the equity derivatives department at UBS Securities in New York, refers to range forwards as zero-cost collars plus a forward contract. As such, the package has three main components: a call, a put and a forward. All three have the same underlying and time to maturity.

The strikes on the call and the put are selected so that the premiums will offset each other. Roughly equidistant from the two strikes is the forward rate, says Avanessians, who notes that "the volatility risk [here] is minor because the purchase of the put is offset by the volatility risk in the sale of the call."

While the underlying in range forwards can be anything from equities to fixed income to commodities, according to Avanessians, they have been used most widely with currencies. Range forwards allow users to take advantage of favorable currency movements up to the high end of the range while limiting risk at the lower end, much like the caps and floors of an interest-rate collar or the put and call options in an equity index zero-cost collar.

One market participant says range forwards are exactly like collars—one of several names by which range forwards are known. The range forward was originally conceived by Salomon Brothers in the mid-1980s. Around the same time, Goldman trademarked the name "Min-Max" for exactly the same structure, according to Avanessians. Among the many names by which this structure is known are cylinder options, forward bands, option fences, risk reversals and tunnels.

Zilberman notes that range forwards reflect a bullish view on the underlying and a desire for downside protection. Corporations which have foreign currency exposures and do not want to miss the bottom of the dollar responded to recent European currency crises by making range forwards extremely popular. But Zilberman notes that the up and downside limits set by the range forward can potentially make for opportunity losses. The alternative to buy a

RANGE FORWARD PAYOFFS

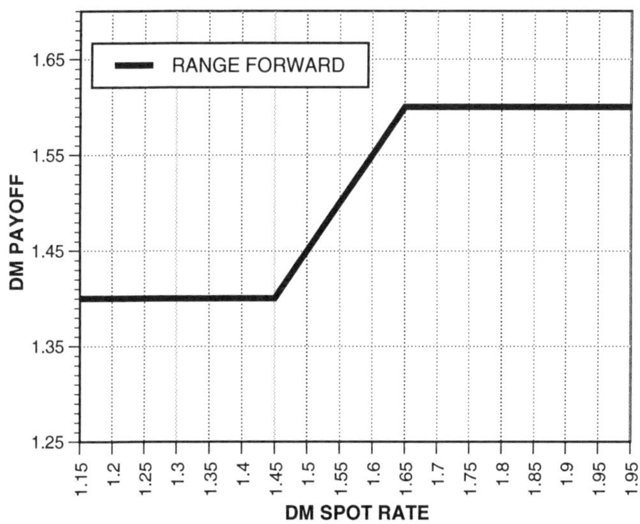

straight option, or when the currency strengthens to buy back the short portion of the range forward, if you take a bullish view of the currency.

As an example of the structure's use in the currency markets, consider an investor who will receive DM10 million in three months and wants to hedge his exposure while gaining the potential upside of the Deutsche mark without paying a premium. The current DM/US$ spot rate is DM1.47 and the current three-month forward is DM1.4930. To guard against DM decline, the investor buys a DM put/US$ call with a strike of DM1.60. The DM put premium is 1.60% of the U.S. dollar underlying ($6.25 million), or $100,000. The investor then sells a DM call/US$ put with a strike price of DM1.40 and a premium of 1.40% of the U.S. dollar underlying ($7.15 million), or $100,000.

> Range forwards reflect a bullish view on the underlying and a desire for downside protection.

If the DM depreciates above the DM/US$ spot rate of DM1.60, the investor would exercise the DM put/U.S. dollar call at 1.60, and the DM call/US$ put expires worthless. The investor earns $6.25 million (DM10 million divided by DM1.60/US$1). If the spot rate is between the strike prices of DM1.40 and DM1.60, neither the DM put nor the DM call is exercised. The investor sells DM at the spot rate. But if DM appreciates below the DM/US$ rate of DM1.40, the investor's DM put expires worthless while the short DM call is exercised against him at DM1.40, which gives the investor $7.15 million (DM10 million divided by DM1.40/US$1.00) (see graph).

Zilberman notes that other variations on the range forward include the "some-cost range forward" where an investor pays a low premium, rather than zero. This enables him to set the strike of the call higher and thus achieve a greater upside potential. Another variation is the "participating range forward" where the investor sells 90% of a call option rather than 100%.

EQUITY PARTICIPATION NOTES

Equity participation notes (EPNs), sometimes known as equity-linked bonds, are bonds which have a coupon or redemption value linked to the performance of a stock or index. EPNs allow investors to gain long-term exposure to a stock or index with reduced risk and reduced principal requirements. They have become popular in recent years as high volatility in stock markets has made retail and institutional investors uncertain about returns. EPNs can have exposure to all major indices, stocks and baskets of stocks, explained Liz Cacciottolo, director-U.K. investor coverage at Swiss Bank Corp. in London.

The typical EPN structure comprises a bond and an embedded option: a zero-coupon bond and a call option, for example. If an investor purchased a five-year zero-coupon bond from a major bank or a corporate issuer with a yield of 8.7% annually, the cost of the bond would be 65.90%. A roughly 66% capital outlay has guaranteed the investor a return of 100%, leaving 34% which can be used to purchase an option to gain exposure to an index. If five-year calls on the FT-SE 100 can be purchased at a cost of 22%, the investor can purchase over one-and-a-half options, thus gaining an upside exposure of 155% to the index.

The structure of the EPN is not set and a wide variety of options can be embedded into the bond, noted Cacciottolo. For example, an embedded quanto option would mean any rise in a foreign index would be converted into the currency of the investor without any negative effect of exchange rate fluctuations. The investor can also get higher return from a foreign index or stock by using a higher yielding currency. An investor could buy a five-year lira zero-coupon bond, for example, with an annual rate of 14.25%. This would mean the bond would cost 51.4%, allowing the investor to spend 48.6% on an option. If the investor could buy a Nikkei quanto option for 28% it would allow him to purchase enough options to give him an upside of 173% of the Nikkei index, Cacciottolo continued.

EPNs can also contain ladder options, locking the investor into a certain percentage rise in a stock or index regardless of whether the underlying falls below the threshold by the next payment date of the EPN, if it has set payment dates over its life, or on the maturity of the product, explains Reny Thabard, head of equity derivatives at Caisse des Dépôts et Consignations in Paris. If, on the other hand, the index has risen, the ladder will lock in the new

AN EQUITY PARTICIPATION NOTE

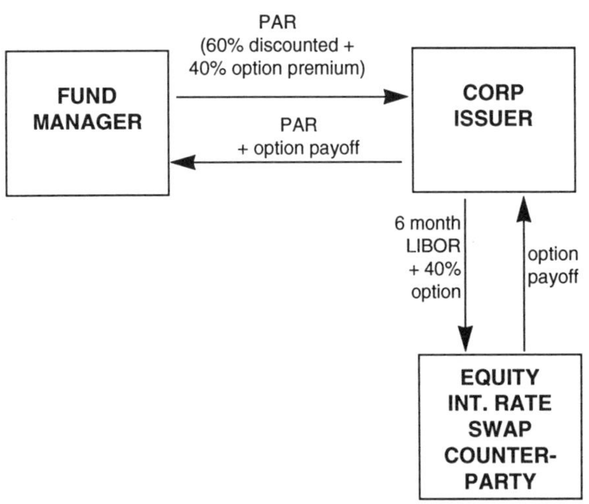

higher value. It is usual for the embedded option to share the same tenor as the bond, and it is exercised automatically, he added.

> The structure of the EPN is not set and a wide variety of options can be embedded into the bond.

A wholesaler, a major banking institution and derivatives player, will create an EPN which is sold by a retail bank, insurance company or building society (the U.K. equivalent of a U.S. savings and loan) to the investor, said Cacciottolo. In the U.S., broker/dealers have seen market demand and then gone to potential bond issuers and shown them the potential benefits of tapping into the market for EPNs, says Ron Slivka, v.p. in the equity derivative group at J.P. Morgan Securities in New York. The broker/dealer will hedge the risk of the option for the issuer, and can reduce the issuer's overall costs of funding as he will make sure that the bond issue and the hedge costs for the embedded option are equal to or less than the costs of a straight bond issue. The broker/dealer can dynamically hedge the embedded options with futures, or with stock baskets and cash, explained Slivka.

In North America, EPNs tend to be custom-made for specific investors so secondary trading is not great, but markets are offered to allow investors to close their positions. This is especially helpful if the EPN is deep in the money, explained Slivka. EPN structures also sometimes offer guaranteed exit prices. If an investor left a three-year EPN at the end of the first year, for example, he could receive back 85% of his original outlay and perhaps 80% of the upside of the index, said Cacciottolo. The minimum guarantee and participation levels will normally increase as the EPN reaches maturity.

The demand for EPNs has been greater in Europe than the U.S. because European investors are traditionally equity-biased, according to Cacciottolo. The idea of EPNs has proven attractive to investors in North America, according to Slivka, although he acknowledged that European investors do demand more complex structures than their U.S. counterparts. This demand for complexity stems partly from European investors' greater experience with over-the-counter-options, as option exchanges developed at a later stage in Europe compared to the U.S., Slivka argued.

SPREAD-LOCK INTEREST RATE SWAPS

A spread-lock interest rate swap enables an investor or issuer to lock in a swap spread and apply it to an interest rate swap executed at some point in the future. This type of swap can be used, for example, by a bond issuer which takes the bearish view that spreads might tighten while looking to pay fixed but is undecided about Treasury rates. Conversely, the swap can also be used by a bullish money manager looking for higher yields that result from widening spreads.

The spread-lock interest rate swap consists of two components: a spread-lock and an interest rate swap. An issuer makes an agreement with the dealer or bank at the outset of the transaction to set a swap spread. They then agree to fix a Treasury rate within an agreed upon time frame, say three months out, or at a point within that time frame when the issuer thinks Treasury rates have bottomed out. Conversely, the investor will fix the Treasury rates when they have risen. The issuer/investor has the choice of setting the Treasury rate in an American or European style. If the issuer/investor fails to set the Treasury rate, the bank sets it at the end of the spread-lock agreement regardless of where the Treasury rate is, says Mark Cahill, first v.p. at Republic National Bank of New York.

The rate and swap spread together equal the fixed rate the issuer/investor will pay the bank for the life of the swap, which in this case begins at the end of the three month spread-lock. The dealer is then obligated to pay the issuer/investor a floating rate, typically three-month LIBOR, according to Armand Tatevossian, director-financial products group at Barclays de Zoete Wedd in New York. Tatevossian also notes that an investor can purchase an option on a swap spread-lock and not be obligated to enter into the swap.

The spread-lock interest rate swap is more of a roll of the dice for the investor than the bank, says Cahill. For instance, suppose an issuer/investor enters into a European-style, three-month expi-

SPREAD-LOCK INTERST RATE SWAP

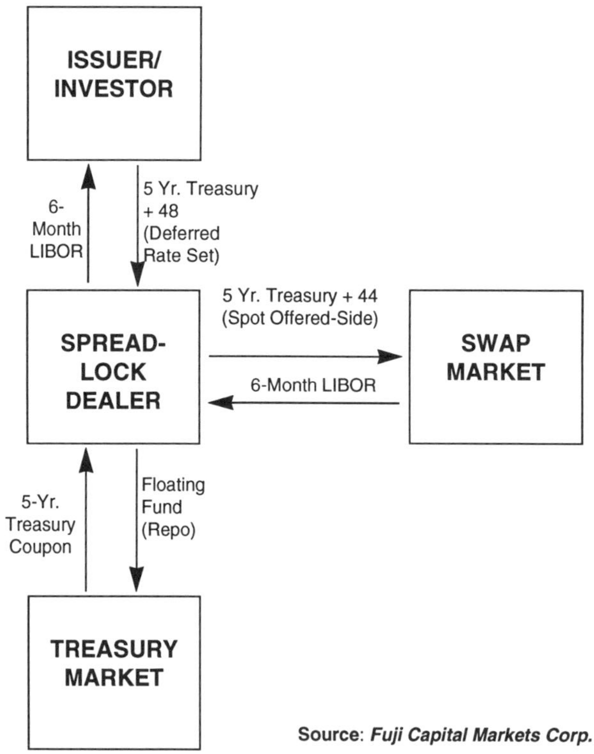

Source: ***Fuji Capital Markets Corp.***

ration spread-lock agreement where he pays fixed and receives floating in a forward-starting, five-year swap. According to Tatevossian, "Essentially, the fair-value locked-in spread is based on the dealer's expected cost of carrying the associated hedge transactions for the three-month period."

> "Essentially, the fair-value locked-in spread is based on the dealer's expected cost of carrying the associated hedge transactions for the three-month period."

Tatevossian says the dealer's spread-lock hedge involves two separate transactions: First, the dealer enters into a spot-start five-year, three-month swap in the swap market where it pays fixed and receives floating (see accompanying chart). The maturity date of this swap matches that of the spread-lock swap. The dealer then purchases the appropriate number of five-year Treasury securities, funded by overnight repo, from the Treasury market. The Treasury hedge is lifted in three months when the spread-lock starts. The cost of the hedge will factor in Treasury roll risk (replacing off-the-run notes with newly issued notes) and repo rate risk, Tatevossian notes.

"The swap trade hedges the spread-lock dealer with respect to changes in the swap spread, and the Treasury transaction hedges the dealer with respect to changes in the five-year Treasury rate," says Tatevossian. "The dealer then computes what the expected cost of these two transactions will be for the three-month period. It is this cost which the dealer must recoup from the spread-lock counterparty over the life of the five-year swap." Which is why the dealer receives from the issuer/investor four basis points more than it pays to the swap market.

VOLATILITY

Volatility is the measure of the degree of uncertainty in a given quantity. That quantity could be the price of an underlying instrument, its yield, or the logarithm of the price or yield. As a guide to risk, volatility is a crucial factor in the pricing of derivatives. Explains Kosrow Dehnad, v.p. in charge of new product development at Chase Securities, volatility can be divided into two distinct types: historical and implied. Historical volatility is arrived at using past economic data, while implied volatility represents market uncertainty at a given instance.

Historical volatility can be estimated by calculating the square root of variance, says Dehnad. Suppose you have three values for your underlying quantity: 1, 2, and 3. The first step to working out the volatility is to find the average of the values, in this case 2. The deviation for each of the values from the average is then calculated and squared so the resultant volatility cannot be negative. For the first observation value the deviation is 1, for the second it is 0, and for the third it is 1. The three results are then added together and divided by the number of observation points minus one (this subtraction avoids mathematical bias in the result). In the above example the standard deviation or historical volatility will be equal to one.

The problem in calculating historical volatility is preventing one large price movement from making the overall result unhelpful. There are many models which allow volatility to be sensitized to "outliers," which can distort volatility results. Trimmed standard deviation method means that the given number of values are ordered from smallest to largest, with a given percentage at either end being discarded. Median Absolute Deviation (MAD) means that if you have five data points with values of: 1,3,6,25,50, then 6 would be your median point, and volatility would be judged from that point.

Implied volatility can appear less scientific but it relies on models used by professionals in their calculations of options pricing. Given that all the other factors in pricing an option—such as strike, maturity and interest rates—are observable or can be defined by the client, implied volatility stands out as representing the unknown, says Dehnad. Market sentiment is therefore key in estimating ranges for implied volatility. The trader will look at particular prices being quoted for an option in the market, and will then run those prices through his own system to see the implied volatility being offered by other professionals. It is then up to him whether to quote higher or lower volatility based on his own judgments on the underlying and its relation to political and economic factors.

In the foreign exchange markets where the systems for pricing options by traders are standardized, there is no controversy over implied volatility, and, in fact, prices are quoted purely in those terms in the professional market. This is not the case in the equity

USD/DM VOLATILITY

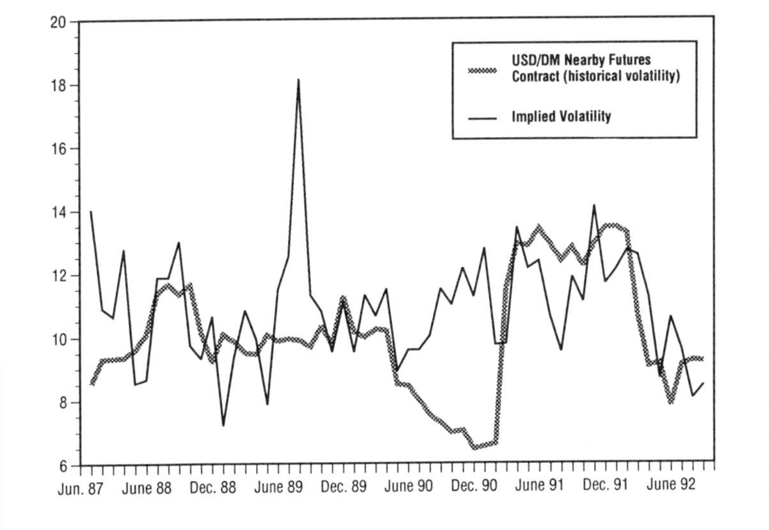

markets where there are fewer standardized models for pricing derivatives. Implied volatility can itself be a reflection of the relative liquidity of certain markets. In a more liquid market, implied volatility will move quickly to reflect the conditions of the underlying market. In contrast, in a quiet market dealers will sell options in the expectation that time decay will mean they will be able to buy them back cheaper, so driving implied volatility down. In less liquid markets, volatilities will also be driven by end-user demand. If clients are only buyers, implied volatility will be high as traders have little opportunity to offset their option risk.

Implied volatility can itself be a reflection of the relative liquidity of certain markets.

For sales teams, judgments between historical and implied volatility are important for advising clients on when to buy and sell options. There are greater rewards for selling options when implied volatility is higher than historical volatility and for buying options when the reverse is the case. High volatility in the underlying means there is a greater risk of price movements resulting in the option ending out-of-the-money. As a consequence an investor will want a higher return, so forcing up premium prices.

Models for estimating implied volatility are becoming more sophisticated, according to Dehnad. At its simplest, if a die is rolled the variability of the outcome can be represented as volatility. But for options structures like a one-year cap, where options will be written with three-month, six-month, nine-month and one-year tenors, the dealer cannot just rest on the possibility of the variability being evenly distributed. There is the possibility that the variability could change, like a die becoming loaded, and so newer models have been developed to take account of this, Dehnad continues.

ASSET-BASED SWAPS

Asset-based swaps are typically transactions that combine a swap with the purchase of a bond, according to Andrew Langerman, managing director at Bear Stearns. Langerman adds that in most asset-based swaps an investor seeks to replace a fixed with a floating rate. By doing so, "investors are able to alter the interest rate and currency sensitivity of their portfolios without having to disturb the underlying pool of assets," explains Armand Tatevossian, v.p. at Barclays Bank in New York. The biggest users of asset swaps are mostly European and Japanese banks, securities firms and insurance companies.

In the mid-1980s, the classic asset-based swap was the risk-controlled arbitrage, which combined mortgage-backed securities such as Ginnie Maes with interest rate swaps, Tatevossian says. He adds that in the last few years investors have used "Japanese ex-warrant issues, bonds with undervalued embedded options and certain CMO [collateralized mortgage obligation] tranches" in asset swaps.

"Asset swappers are continuously scanning the Eurobond markets to find bonds trading at a discount or paying a high enough coupon to yield an above-LIBOR rate after a swap," Tatevossian says. He explains that "in the aftermath of the [1992] European Rate Mechanism currency crisis and selective credit downgradings, certain European sovereign debt (e.g. Kingdom of Spain and Italy) and Eurobond corporates (e.g. Canadians) traded down to a price level sufficient to meet or exceed the asset-swap yield target of European bank clients, typically around 20 to 25 basis points above LIBOR."

The cumulative effect of a large number of Deutsche mark-denominated debt issues, coupled with the swaps done by the issuers, narrowed DM swap spreads from 45 basis points to eight basis points, spurring a boom in the asset swap business.

Typically in asset-based swaps a fixed-rate bond is transformed into a synthetic, floating-rate asset through an interest rate swap, according to John Doherty, head of the asset swaps desk at Bankers Trust in New York. For instance, an investor owns a XYZ corporate bond bought at par, which generates a fixed coupon of 9% paid semi-annually, and thinks rates will rise within the next six months and therefore wants protection against a decline in the bond price (see illustration). Rather than sell the XYZ corporate bond and buy a floating rate instrument, the investor enters into an interest rate swap with a bank whereby the investor pays the bank the fixed rate of 4.5% every six months and receives from the bank LIBOR plus 50 basis points.

As an example of a currency-based asset swap, Daniel Seymour, senior associate in global swaps and options at Barclays Bank in New York, cites an investor who buys a five-year, Finnish bond denominated in Deutsche marks, worth DM10 million and paying an annual coupon of 7.5%. The investor wants to receive his

FIXED TO FLOATING ASSET SWAP

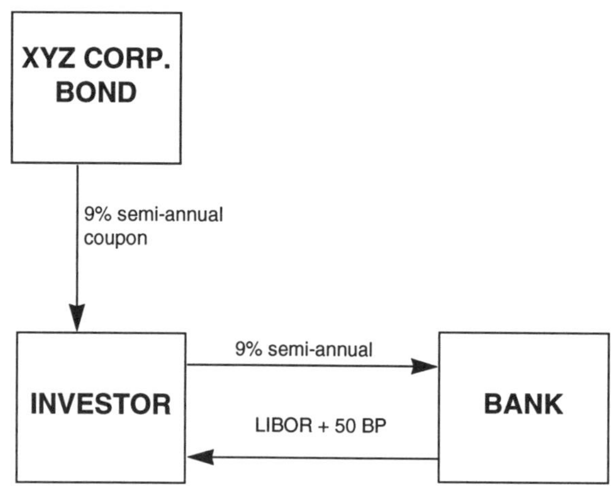

Source: ***Bankers Trust***

returns in dollars because the investor feels the dollar is stronger than the Deutsche mark.

First, the investor and the swap dealer exchange principal amounts at the spot exchange rate, say US$1=DM1.67, in which case the bank pays the investor $6 million while the investor pays the bank DM10 million. Assuming that the payment dates for the bond and the swap are the same, the periodic currency interest rates are such that the investor pays annual interest rate payments to the bank of DM750,000 and receives from the bank semi-annual payments at a floating rate of U.S. dollar LIBOR plus 30 basis points, for example. At maturity, the investor and the bank exchange principal amounts at the initial DM/US$ spot rate (US$1=DM1.67) to complete the transaction.

> With asset swaps, "investors are able to alter the interest rate and currency sensitivity of their portfolios without having to disturb the underlying pool of assets."

Though the transaction is straightforward, asset-based swaps are not without risks. "If the underlying asset fails to perform, the investor may have to sell or unwind the interest-rate swap at the market rate, potentially absorbing a capital loss," says Tatevossian. "In addition, the investor has assumed credit risk on the asset swap counterparty for the life of the swap." He also notes that asset swap packages containing callable bonds or mortgages should be combined with a puttable swap to protect against the bond being called or the mortgage being prepaid if interest rates fall.

Finally, as with most derivative products, assets swap come in numerous permutations. For instance, assuming the asset is a bond, there are payoff variations on how the asset swap functions in relation to whether the bond trades at par, at a discount or at a premium, says Mark Koenigsberg, director of emerging markets research at Salomon Brothers. Likewise, the asset on which the transaction is based does not have to be a straight coupon bond. It can very well be a zero coupon bond, a privately issued bond or an equity-linked bond, according to Frank Ronan, managing director-swaps at Merrill Lynch Capital Markets in New York.

DURATION

The measurement of duration is critical for portfolio managers and derivatives players hedging and speculating in the fixed-income markets. At its simplest, modified duration is approximated by the percentage change in price of a one basis point move in the yield of a fixed-income instrument, while dollar duration is the actual change in price for a one percentage point change in yield, explains Jim Durrant, head of research at Paribas Capital Markets. Differing maturity instruments will have different duration values, and, thus, portfolio managers will have to hedge themselves accordingly.

Modified duration is derived from Macaulay duration, according to Durrant. Macaulay duration is the length of time in which you would receive half of the cash flows on a bond in present value terms. Modified duration, however, is not considered as a unit of time, and is arrived at by the following formula:

Macaulay Duration/(1+Y/n)

where Y is the yield to maturity of the bond, and n is the number of coupon payments per year, explains Durrant. Macaulay duration is not as effective a concept for bond investors because it does not tell them precisely how sensitive a bond is to a change in yield, unlike modified and dollar duration, Durrant explained.

In a 10% annual flat yield curve environment, the value of a one basis point move in yield would be 0.9 for a one-year security, 1.73 for a two-year, 2.49 for a three-year and 3.17 for a four-year, says Ed Charles, v.p.-investor derivatives marketing at J.P. Morgan in London. If the investor has $100 million worth of two-year securities, $50 million of three-year securities and $75 million of four-year securities, the total value of change if yields shift in parallel by one basis point would be $53,450 (the individual volumes multiplied by the price value of a one basis point shift in yield). A portfolio manager may decide to hedge that exposure using single maturity futures such as 10-year contracts. The duration on a 10-year bond is approximately 6.14 in the context of a flat yield curve of 10% annually, so the portfolio manager could be perfectly hedged by shorting just over $87 million notional of 10-year futures (53,450 divided by .00614), Charles explains.

As an overlay manager, TSA Capital Management in Los Angeles must determine duration of the futures contracts it uses in order to match it with the dollar duration of the underlying, explains David Depew, principal and head of trading at the firm. Futures duration will be based on the duration of the underlying bond most likely to be delivered against the contract, Depew continues. The futures contract will be run through a system to gauge possible yield changes and hence possible changes in the cheapest to deliver bond against the contract in order to arrive at the instrument's duration, Depew explained.

PRICE/YIELD GRAPH FOR 10 YEAR 8% BOND

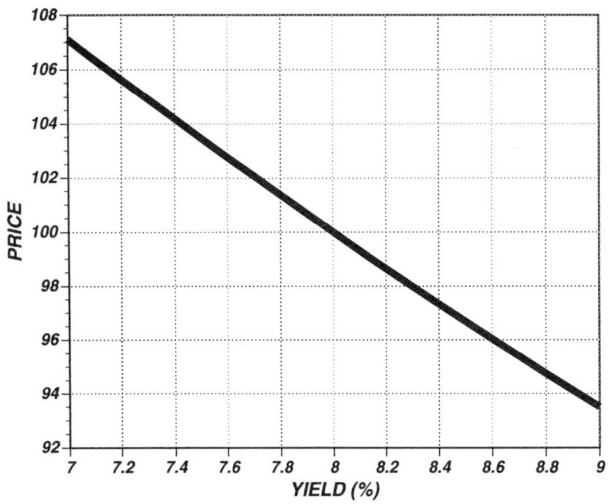

Duration can also be used in hedging swaps by splitting up a transaction's component parts, explains Charles. For example, in a fixed to floating swap in a 10% annual flat rate yield environment, the fixed leg can be considered as a bond paying an annual coupon, so for a 10-year swap it would have a modified duration of around 6.14. The floating leg of the swap can be considered as a floating rate note, Charles continues. If the first cash flow from the floating leg will be in six months, then the floating rate note can be considered as a six-month zero-coupon bond. The duration for the hypothetical floating rate note will be 0.5, says Charles. Thus, the netted out duration on the swap would be equal to 5.64 (6.14-0.5). So if the swap counterparties are expecting parallel movements in the yield curves, they can adjust their duration weightings.

> The measurement of duration is critical for portfolio managers and derivatives players hedging and speculating in the fixed-income markets.

Duration theory is limited because it assumes that yield shifts are parallel for differing maturities and that the yield curve itself is flat, says Durrant. But even if a portfolio manager is taking a view that yield curves will not move in parallel, duration is still a useful concept, he adds. The portfolio manager may expect short yields to fall more quickly than long yields. Thus, he could enter into two swaps where he received three-year fixed and paid 10-year fixed, Durrant explains. The principal of the three-year swap would have to be greater than the notional principal of the 10-year swap in order to be immune to parallel yield curve shifts, he continued.

Derived from duration is the concept of convexity. Convexity refers to the degree of curvature of the price yield graph, where the x-axis is the yield, the y-axis is the price and the slope itself is the duration (see graph). Duration can be considered analogous to delta in options, and convexity analogous to gamma, explains Durrant.

Convexity is either positive or negative. Positive convexity means that as the price increases, the duration of the instruments will increase likewise. Negative convexity means that when the price increases the duration decreases. As the bond market trades higher, TSA benefits its customers by swapping its long position in bond futures for call options on the futures, according to Depew. This strategy is utilized as long bond futures have negative convexity, while bond options have positive convexity. Bond futures have a negative convexity, as they track the cheapest to deliver bond.

CMT-BASED DERIVATIVES

The constant-maturity Treasury (CMT) yield "can be thought of as a yield on a bond that doesn't age," explains Mark Koenigsberg, director of emerging markets research at Citicorp in New York. This yield can be used as a reference rate for derivative products such as yield curve swaps and CMT-linked caps and floors. The CMT rate attracts investors who want exposure to a particular point on the Treasury yield curve.

CMT yields are calculated daily by the U.S. Treasury to determine its cost of funds. Each trading day at 3:30 p.m. Eastern Standard Time, the Federal Reserve collects bids on Treasury yields for nearly all maturities (six months, one year, two, three, five, 10 and 30 years) from five institutions out of a rotating pool of 39 primary dealers in U.S. government securities. The Fed averages the bid yields on the on-the-run (or current) and off-the-run (or older, outstanding) Treasury securities, with on-the-runs receiving more weight, and then plots a smooth curve through the Treasury yields for each of the maturities. The estimated CMT rates are published every Monday by the Fed and are available on Telerate.

Because CMT rates are yields on bonds that do not age, the yields no longer "roll down the yield curve." Michael Kastner, v.p. and options strategist at Société Générale in New York, notes that—given an absence of yield curve movement—an investor holding a two-year note yielding 4.62% would after three months be holding a 21-month security with a yield of, say, 4.50%. The rate, therefore, would have rolled down the yield curve slightly.

According to Kastner, "If an investor wants to initiate a position on the two-year note [for instance], but not be subjected to the effects of rolling down the yield curve, he would be interested in a CMT[-linked]" security. For example, Kastner notes that caps on CMTs are "especially attractive to someone interested in employing the two-year note as a vehicle to profit from an anticipated Fed tightening."

If the investor is more concerned about declining interest rates, CMT-linked derivatives can play a role too. Armand Tatevossian, director of the global swaps and options group at Barclays Bank in New York, explains that "as interest rates have declined, mortgage-backed security [MBS] portfolios have become cash-laden due to high prepayment levels; some investors have chosen to lock in some minimal reinvestment rate by purchasing floors on the CMT 10-year rate."

Tatevossian offers the example of an investor faced with prepayment risk on a portfolio of mortgage-backed securities. The investor, he says, pays an upfront premium for $10 million

FORWARD CURVE FOR LIBOR 5-YR. AND 10-YR. CONSTANT-MATURITY TREASURIES

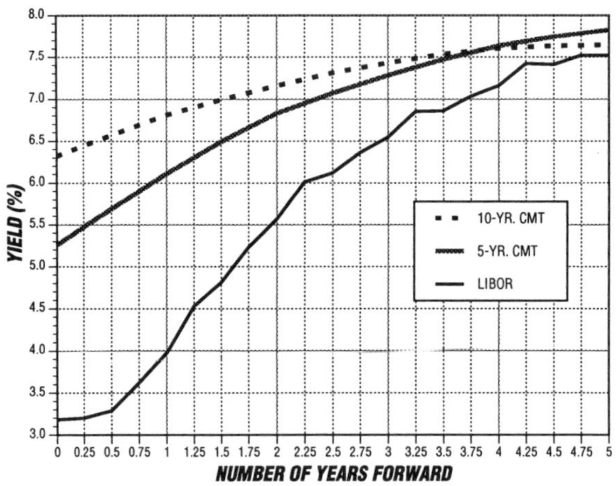

(notional) of three-year floors referenced to the CMT 10-year index, currently at 6.80%, and chooses a strike rate of 6.50%, paid semi-annually in arrears. If in six months the 10-year CMT rate has declined to 6.00%, the first fixing of the floor will be in the money, and the CMT floor dealer must pay the investor $25,277 or (182 days/360 days) x $10 million x 6.50%-6.00%.

CMT caps are especially attractive to someone interested in employing the two-year note as a vehicle to profit from an anticipated Fed tightening.

In terms of option pricing, Tatevossian further adds, "As a plain-vanilla LIBOR floor is priced with the expectation that future LIBOR rates will trace the LIBOR forward curve, the price of a 10-year CMT floor is similarly based on the expectation that the future 10-year CMT rates will trace the forward 10-year Treasury curve." He adds that, given a steep U.S. dollar Treasury curve, the forward rate curve implied for longer-term CMT indexes will be significantly higher and flatter than those of shorter-term CMT indexes (see illustration).

Finally, Tatevossian explains that the price of a three-year CMT floor depends on the dealer's expected hedging costs, which are associated with creating dynamically hedged call option positions on 10-year Treasury notes. Because the three-year CMT floor, for example, has five semi-annual fixings, it is similar to a portfolio of five Treasury call options on the then current 10-year Treasury note, he says. He adds that the notional amount of each call option roughly equals $10 million times the ratio of the modified durations of a six-month Treasury over a 10-year Treasury ($0.735 million = $10 million x [0.5 years/6.8 years]).

FORWARD INTEREST RATES

A forward interest rate curve shows what the interest rate will be at a given time in the future. Forward rates are an important element both in prompting use of derivatives and in pricing such derivative products as interest rate swaps, caps and floors. For example, in a fixed to floating swap, the fixed rate is based on the assumption that the expected floating leg payments will be the forward rates that prevail at the time of transaction, according to Kosrow Dehnad, v.p. in charge of new product development at Chase Securities.

Given the prevailing rates and prices for financial instruments in the market, forward rates are determined in such a way to prevent any arbitrage opportunity, explains Dehnad. For example, suppose the current three-month and six-month LIBOR rates are f3 and f6, respectively. If f is three-month LIBOR three months forward, then it must satisfy the following equation:

$$(1 + f3 \times \text{days deposited}/360) \times$$
$$(1 + f \times \text{days deposited}/360)$$
$$=$$
$$(1 + f6 \times \text{days deposited}/360)$$

This relationship can be used to determine f, the three month forward rate.

In other words, $1 invested at the three-month LIBOR rate for three months and then compound reinvested for a further three months at the three-month forward rate must be equal to investing

$1 for six months at the six-month LIBOR rate. If the forward rate violates this condition then arbitrage opportunities arise, continues Dehnad. As yield is a factor in determining forward rates, a steep yield curve will result in a steep forward curve, he said.

The forward rate can also be arrived at using futures contracts such as Eurodollar futures, continues Dehnad. The settlement of those contracts is based on the LIBOR rate two days prior to expiration, so market participants are buying or selling on where they expect rates to be at that time. To determine a forward rate for a date that falls between two contracts, one can use interpolation. For example, linear interpolation takes a weighted sum of the rates of the two closest contracts to the date of interest, with the closer contract carrying more weight. Linear interpolation is not perfect, however, because rates at year-end ('turn') tend to be higher than those after the new year, so more refined methods have been devised to determine forward rates.

One application of forward rates is in determining the fixed leg

6 MONTH LIBOR U.S. FORWARD RATES as of November 17, 1992

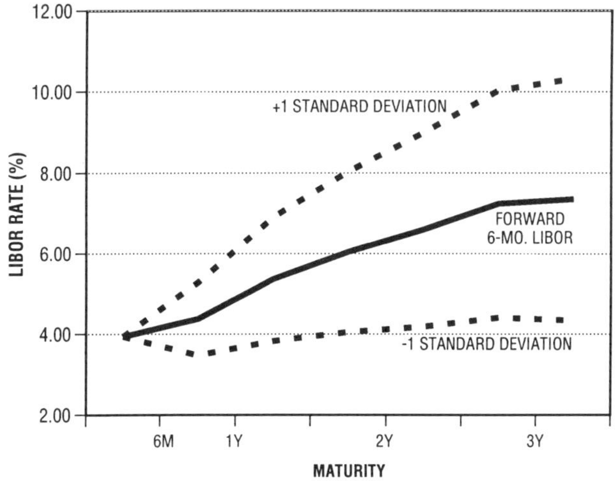

of an interest rate swap. The fixed rate is determined in such a way that the stream of fixed coupon payments and the floating coupon payments (the forward rates) would have the same values. The forward curve is also important in pricing of caps and floors and other fixed-income options, says Neil Dodgson, associate director at National Westminster Capital Markets. For example, if a corporation wishes to buy an eight-year 9% cap, the writer of the cap needs to know the forward rate eight years out to see the possibility of how deep in or out of the money the cap will be in order to arrive at the intrinsic value of the cap. This intrinsic value will be taken into account with the volatility of the option in order to price the cap.

> Forward rates are an important element both in prompting use of derivatives, and in pricing such derivative products as interest rate swaps, caps and floors.

The differing forward rates for currencies also form the basis for differential swaps, where one counterparty pays a floating interest of one currency and receives floating in another, with both payments denominated in the same currency, explains Dehnad.

The forward curve does not hold a preponderant position for swappers, however. Each house will have a different, proprietary basis for the pricing of their swaps and options. Lloyds Treasury Products in London prices swaps based on the futures curve rather than on the forward rate curve, explains Megan Frost, senior manager. This is done because the group runs an integrated forward rate agreement and swap book which is hedged using futures. The problem in this strategy is the further one proceeds out on the futures curve, the less reliable futures are as a means of pricing, as the long-tenor futures market has less depth, she says. So, three years out there is an overlap in Lloyd's use of the futures curve and the gilt yield curve for pricing swaps, Frost continued.

But forward curves do play an important part in swap pricing, says Dodgson. The fact that each swap and option house will have its own system generating forward curves also opens up the possibility of interesting arbitrage opportunities, he continued. According to Dehnad, forward rates are supposed to be unbiased estimators of future rates, but they do tend to overestimate or underestimate future rates for consecutive periods. Forward rates are positively autocorrelated, that is, if forward rates are overestimated for one period, they are overestimated for the next period. But a combination of forward rates and implied volatility can enable market participants to determine a "confidence interval," a range within which they think future rates will fall (see figure), rather than using forward rates alone, which are point estimates.

OPTIONS ON SPREADS

A spread option is an option in which the payoff formula, rather than being a function of a single price or yield, is a function of the difference between two prices or yields, according to Daniel Seymour, senior associate-debt capital markets at Barclays de Zoete Wedd in New York. Referring to options on spreads as "correlation options," Kosrow Dehnad, v.p. in charge of new product development at Chase Securities in New York, says spread options are "the wave of the future" because they allow investors, for instance, to act on their view of how two instruments—such as two rates on the yield curve—will move with respect to each other.

According to Sean Huang, v.p.-trading and risk management at Mitsubishi Capital Market Services, options on spreads come in a nearly infinite variety, some of which include options on yield curve spreads, money market spreads—commercial paper, prime, LIBOR, T-bill and Eurodollar futures—as well as spreads in the mortgage, swap, commodity, currency and hybrid (i.e. equity and bond) markets. More often than not, spread option buyers and sellers—including money managers, pension funds and dealers—take a directional view on a specific spread.

Options on spreads can also be used as hedging vehicles. An investor with exposure to a spread, for instance, might buy a spread option as a hedge, while an investor with a view on spread changes might use an option to speculate, according to Leon Tatevossian, v.p.-derivatives research at Salomon Brothers in New York. Tatevossian notes that options on spreads "are natural vehicles for investors who want to take positions on inter-government interest rate differentials." As an example, he offers what some traders have called an "outperformance" or "better performance" option.

In this example, Tatevossian explains that an investor who believes that the Japanese bond market will underperform the U.S. bond market (in yield terms) can implement this view by buying a put option on the inter-government yield spread. If, for example, the yield on the benchmark Japanese 10-year bond stands at 4.80%, while the yield on the on-the-run U.S. Treasury 10-year note is at 6.81%, there is a 201 basis point differential. Where U is equal to the yield on the U.S. Treasury note and J is equal to the yield of the Japanese Government bond, the put option's payoff formula would be: (FACE AMOUNT) x MAX [0, 201-(U-J)]. In this example, the strike of the put option is the starting yield spread, which is 201.

If U-J settles above 201, the option expires worthless, and if it is below 201, the investor earns a payoff. Thus, if U-J is 190, the payoff is then 11 basis points times the face amount of $1 million, for

HISTORICAL SPREAD OF 2-YR. TSY VS. 10-YR. TSY

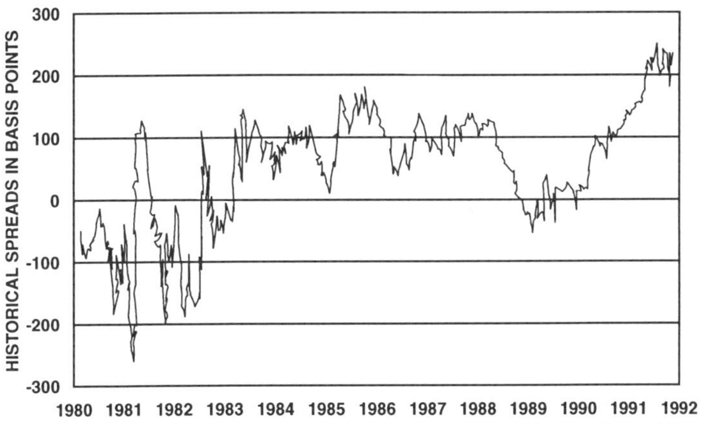

Source: *Chase Securities*

example, which would make for a payoff of $1,100.

"The advantage of this structure is that the investor's payoff is strictly a function of the terminal interest rate differential," Tatevossian explains. "It is not affected by changes in the yen/U.S. dollar exchange rate. Purchasing this customized product is easier than trying to replicate spread exposure by managing a position in the underlying bonds and the currency."

> "The advantage of this structure is that the investor's payoff is strictly a function of the terminal interest rate differential."

Dehnad notes that pricing this customized product calls for sophistication and sound judgment, for the process requires more art than science. One market source explains that some of the elements that enter into a dealer's pricing model include: 1) the forward prices (or yields) of the two underlying instruments; 2) the instruments' (price or yield) volatility, and 3) the correlation between changes in the prices or yields.

The art and the judgment involved in pricing options on spreads come into play when the dealer evaluates the correlation between the prices (or yields) by analyzing their history and the prevailing market. Dehnad says the dealer must consider whether to model how the spread itself moves (see illustration) or model the movement of the two underlying assets and look at the spread as a byproduct. "Each approach has an implication regarding how you come up with the volatility of both instruments and their correlation," Dehnad says.

The market source notes that the correlation, which ranges from -1 to +1, is key to pricing an option on a spread. In general, correlation closer to +1 implies less variability in the spread and, therefore, a lower option price. "An estimate for the correlation can be obtained by analyzing the history of two individual yields," explains Tatevossian.

LIBOR-IN-ARREARS SWAPS

LIBOR-in-arrears swaps are similar to plain vanilla swaps except that the floating rate for each period of the swap is set at the end of the payment period rather than at the beginning, according to Karen Onderko, v.p.-derivative products group at Banque Indosuez in New York. LIBOR-in-arrears swaps are particularly attractive in steeply positive or negative yield curve environments, explains Onderko. The structure is also known as a delayed LIBOR reset swap or back-end set swap.

A LIBOR-in-arrears swap is priced using a series of forwards, similar to a plain vanilla swap, except that the forward rates used to determine the cash flows are those one step out on the curve, according to James Bolton, a swaps trader at Westdeutsche Landesbank in New York.

For example, in a straight two-year against three-month LIBOR swap, the flow at three months is determined by the rate from spot to three months, the flow at six months is determined by the three months to six months forward rate, and so on out to the flow at two years which is determined by the forward rate from 21 to 24 months. The in-arrears swap differs in that the flow at three months is determined by the three months against six month forward rate, the flow at six months by the six months against nine months forward, and so on until the final flow at two years, which is determined by the 24 against 27 month forward rate, Bolton said.

The difference in the price between a plain vanilla swap and a LIBOR-in-arrears swap is approximately the difference between the front three-month period and the forward rate for the last arrears set (24 against 27 months), amortized over the term of the swap. In a positively sloped curve this means that the fixed rate payer will have to pay higher rates because he is theoretically receiving the higher LIBOR rate, explains Bolton. The swap can be hedged by buying futures at the short-end and selling futures at the long-end of the swap, as the LIBOR level will be determined then, according to Mark Starr, v.p. and head of institutional derivative origination at Chase Manhattan Bank in New York.

The increase of interest in LIBOR-in-arrears swaps represents a second renaissance for the structure which arrived in the late 1980s, according to Starr. At the time corporate treasurers had mixed feelings about the product because interest rates subsequently jumped, but increased sophistication now means that LIBOR-in-arrears swaps have a much broader user base.

LIBOR-in-arrears swaps are particularly timely because of the steep yield curve environment in the U.S. and the negative yield curve in many European countries, explains Onderko. The product is also attractive because of the increased uncertainty which is being expressed regarding the reliability of the forward rate curve, from which swaps are priced.

Recent studies have led people to voice concern over the predictive ability of forward rates. Those swappers who do not believe

STRAIGHT VS. LIBOR-IN-ARREARS SWAPS

	Fixed Rate Receivable*		
Maturity	Coupon Swap	LIA (3 months)	LIA (6 months)
1 Year	4.07%	4.485%	4.95%
2 Years	4.91	5.27	5.65
3 Years	5.54	5.85	6.17

*rates are as of 12/9/92

Source: ***BNP Capital Markets***

that short-term rates will rise as much as forward rates project should be interested in receiving the fixed rate in exchange for paying LIBOR set in arrears, Onderko said. Swappers will benefit from using the LIBOR-in-arrears structure if they believe the forward rate curve will flatten, or that interest rates will remain the same or decline, according to Starr.

Swappers will benefit from using the LIBOR-in-arrears structure if they believe the forward rate curve will flatten, or that interest rates will remain the same or decline.

In the U.S., the LIBOR-in-arrears swap allows the gap between the fixed rate and LIBOR to be widened, according to Onderko. The fixed rate in LIBOR-in-arrears swaps is greater than for a normal coupon swap, and there are higher fixed rates for swappers who enter into LIBOR-in-arrears swaps against six-month LIBOR rather than against three-month LIBOR (see figure), she continued.

The LIBOR-in-arrears structure also provides opportunities for issue-driven swappers, who wish to receive fixed to pay the coupon to their investors, according to Starr. For example, a two-year against six-month LIBOR-in-arrears swap (i.e. two-year fixed rate with LIBOR set every six months) might allow an issuer to gain sub-LIBOR funding if wide fixed rate spreads are offered to compensate floating payers in a steep yield curve environment, he continued.

EURODOLLAR FUTURES CONTRACTS

Exchange-traded Eurodollar futures contracts, which do not require actual physical delivery of a time deposit, are cash settled and based on the rate at which three-month Eurodollar time deposit funds are offered by major banks in London, notes Armand Tatevossian, director-global swaps and options group at Barclays Bank in New York.

Eurodollar futures contracts are linked to LIBOR so that at a specified date in four three-month intervals the LIBOR and Eurodollar futures rates converge and become one (see illustration). This convergence creates a yield from which one can extrapolate forward rates to price swaps and forward rate agreements, according to Peter Robert, managing director-derivatives group at Bear Stearns in New York.

Tatevossian adds that the contract, having seen rapid growth in the past few years and being closely associated with the dollar swap market, is used by investors and borrowers to protect interest income or expense. Each contract, marked-to-market daily by the exchanges in Singapore, London and Chicago, covers a face amount of $1 million for a three-month interest accrual period. Dexter Charles, senior v.p. and manager of the derivatives trading desk at Chase Securities in New York, notes that the expiration cycle for Eurodollar futures contracts extends for five years with 20 contracts available on a March-June-September-December cycle.

Charles adds that the first year of Eurodollar futures contracts, called the front contracts—or those closest to expiration—have the most liquidity. The contracts for subsequent years, known respectively as red, green, blue and gold contracts, are increasingly less liquid. The gold contracts, currently running from March '97-December '97, just recently started trading, Charles says. Tatevossian notes that the later dated, or back-end, contracts are used primarily by dealers to hedge their swap and cap/floor books.

The Eurodollar futures contract is quoted at a price which is equal to 100 minus the annualized futures yield, expressed as a money market rate. For example, the December '92 contract, whose last trading day was last Monday, settled two London business days before the third Wednesday of the December contract month at a price of 96.37 and a yield of 3.23%. Tatevossian adds that "although the Eurodollar time deposit cash market trades on the basis of yield, the price convention of Eurodollar futures is consistent with the pricing of existing interest rate contracts such that prices rise when interest rates fall and vice versa."

3 MONTH LIBOR VS. SEPTEMBER EURODOLLAR FUTURES CONTRACT

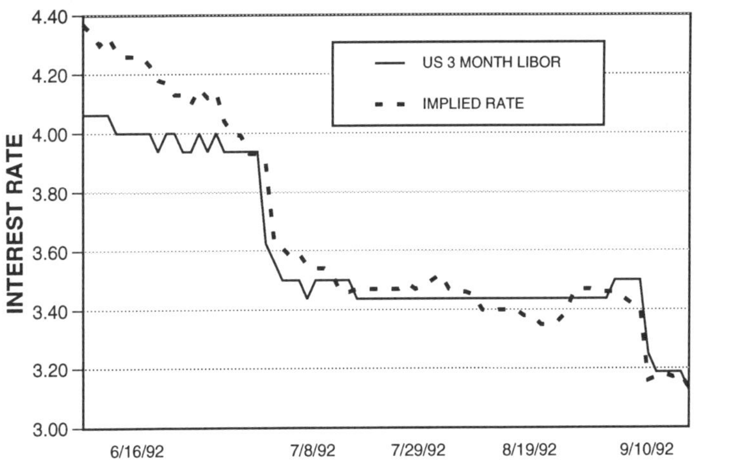

Source: ***Chase Manhattan Futures***

Eurodollar futures contracts can be used to price Eurodollar-based financial instruments, such as swaps and forward rate agreements, with tenors of up to five years. The pricing of longer maturity instruments is done by calculating the implied longer maturity rate from the sequence of shorter maturity rates to produce the Eurodollar strip rate curve, which is used to price swaps, Tatevossian explains. He defines the Eurodollar strip rate as the rate of return which can be realized by an investor placing $1 at the LIBOR rate which corresponds to the maturity of the nearby Eurodollar futures contract. The earnings of this initial investment are then compounded each quarter at the LIBOR rates that are implied by the sequence of futures prices.

Eurodollar futures contracts can be used to price Eurodollar-based financial instruments, such as swaps and forward rate agreements.

"The Eurodollar futures curve, along with the cash LIBOR rate out to the first maturity date, provides the information needed to build a Eurodollar strip rate yield curve," says Tatevossian. For example, assume that on December 1, 1992, the LIBOR rate for a deposit to the settlement at the December 1992 contract (December 16, 1992) is 4.00%. The December 1992 Eurodollar futures contract is trading at a price of 95.80, which implies a yield of 4.2%. The Eurodollar strip rate for the period December 1, 1992, through the maturity of the December 1992 contract (March 17, 1993) is calculated as: 1 + s x 106 (the number of days between Dec. 1 and March 17)/360 (the actual day count basis) = (1 + 0.0400 x 15/360) x (1 + 0.0420 x 91/360) or 4.177%.

This rate can then be used to determine the forward rate all along the yield curve for as long as five years. This yield curve, in turn, is used by dealers to price a variety of swaps. Tatevossian explains that the forward rate makes it possible to calculate the expected floating rate swap cash flows by multiplying the notional amount of the swap by the forward rate which is adjusted by the numbers of days or fractions of a year.

Market-makers use the three-month Eurodollar futures contract to price forward rate agreements, which is a rate two parties agree will be received in the future, says Tatevossian. He notes that the actual amount paid or received is computed by taking the difference between the rate on the contract settlement date and the agreed upon contract rate. The difference is multiplied by the face amount and the term of the deposit. A borrower that is seeking protection from a rate increase would buy an FRA and the party seeking protection from declining rates would sell FRAs.

BREAK FORWARDS

A break forward is a futures instrument which replicates the payoff an investor would achieve if he had purchased a plain vanilla option, according to Jim Durrant, head of research at Paribas Capital Markets. But unlike a vanilla option, no premium is paid upfront for the structure, he continued. The break forward is also known as a delayed premium option.

The break forward differs from a contingent premium option, which also does not require a premium upfront explains Mike Greene, manager of new products at Royal Bank of Canada in London. The break forward investor is required to pay for the option on expiration, regardless of whether it is in- or out-of-the money. With a contingent premium, the option buyer only pays a premium if the option finishes in-the-money.

The break forward is attractive to corporates because the option premium is equivalent to that of a plain vanilla option, explains Durrant. A contingent premium option on the other hand has a premium which is roughly double in price, according to Durrant. The instrument is also attractive to end-users who want to link the use of an option to a specific trade and do not want to pay premium upfront because of particular tax obligations they may be encountering, Greene says.

If a corporate wishes to buy a break forward on a bond, the future value of the option is taken into account, says Durrant. If the current value of the bond stands at 100, and the one-month forward price of the bond is 100.5, a one-month call option with a strike of 100.5 might be worth 0.69%, he continues. The future value of the one-month option has to be calculated as no premium is paid up front for the break forward. This is calculated by taking account of interest rates. Thus the one-month future value of the option premium would be worth 0.7%.

If the price of the bond in one month is worth more than 100.5, the investor is able to buy the bond at the strike plus the premium, Durrant says. If the price of the bond in one month is below the strike, the investor then buys the bond at that value plus the premium level for the out-of-the money call option, he continues.

As the break forward means that an investor does not have to pay a premium upfront, the forward price he is quoted will be less favorable than the 'on-market' or regular price, explains Bryan Thomas, head of exchange options at Bank of America in London. A corporate wanting to buy dollars with sterling in the three-

BREAK FORWARD VS. FORWARD HEDGE

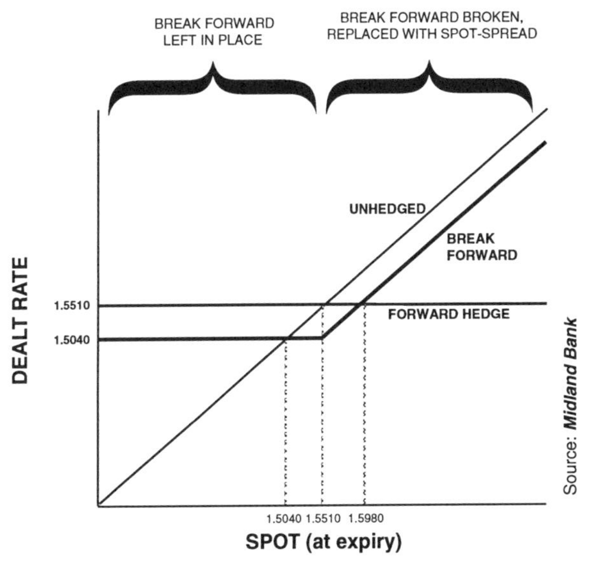

month forward market would be quoted, for example, a price of $1.5510 for £1. But if the corporate was to use the break forward structure the quoted price would probably only be $1.5040 for £1, as the writer of the option has to take account of the premium and the lost interest on it. The 4.7 cents difference between the two offered rates therefore represents the deferred premium, Thomas continues (see graph).

Although the main use of break forwards has been in the currency markets, they can be used on almost any underlying.

In the above example a weakening dollar would result in the option expiring worthless, but the break forward structure means that the corporate can deal at the spot price minus the deferred premium, he explains, which can be considered a breakage fee.

The break forward structure is hedged using the same techniques as are used for plain vanilla options, explains Durrant. Because the writer of the break forward has not received a premium, the position will be hedged by borrowing in the money market, said Greene. There is a small amount of credit risk for the option writer, as he has effectively lent the premium level to the purchaser of the break forward, explains Durrant.

Although the main use of break forwards has been in the currency markets, they can be used on almost any underlying, says Durrant. But as taxation penalties against options have decreased in general and the sophistication of end-users has increased, the break forward's day may have passed, explains Greene.

According to Durrant, the structure still has validity. Some corporates are reluctant to pay premiums as they feed directly into the profit and loss account. The break forward allows corporations that do not have the accounting structure to handle options premiums to take advantage of the options markets, said Thomas.

RAINBOW OPTIONS

Rainbow options are options whose payoff on the exercise date depends on the performance of two or more variables or assets, according to Emanuel Derman, v.p.-head of the quantitative strategies group at Goldman Sachs & Co. Rainbow options can be created using indices such as the DAX or financial instruments such as commodities, adds Kosrow Dehnad, v.p. in charge of new product development at Chase Securities. In addition, Armand Tatevossian, director-financial products group at Barclays de Zoete Wedd in New York, points out that rainbow options allow investors to take a view on the correlation between the component assets.

Gary Gastineau, director-customer risk management research at the investment banking arm of Swiss Bank Corp., defines rainbow options as outperformance options. He notes that they are known by several other names such as multi-index, relative performance and Margrabe options—the latter named for William Margrabe, v.p. in derivatives research at Salomon Brothers, who in March 1978 created the formula used to price the option to exchange one asset for another, Tatevossian says.

To explain how a rainbow option can include several assets, Tatevossian offers the example of an international equity portfolio manager who wants to buy the right to receive a payoff based on the better performance of the German DAX and the French CAC-40—in which case an investor would have a two-color rainbow option. Similarly, by adding Britain's FT-SE 100 to the DAX and the CAC-40, one would have a three-color rainbow option, and so on. Meanwhile, Derman notes that convertible bonds are naturally good examples of two-color rainbow options because the bonds act like an option.

By using commodities Dehnad more clearly shows how rainbow options function between two variables, in this case assets and liabilities. He cites, for example, a gold company that borrows floating rate money to expand operations and hedges its interest rate exposure (liability) by buying a cap. It then overhedges by buying a floor against falling gold (asset) prices instead of more appropriately buying a call on the spread between the price of gold and interest rates.

Both Derman and Tatevossian note a scarcity of investor interest in rainbow options, but Derman says they are of interest to an investor who is the natural owner of an asset and is looking for an elegant way of transforming his position into an investment in

CALL OPTION ON THE MAXIMUM OF TWO STOCKS

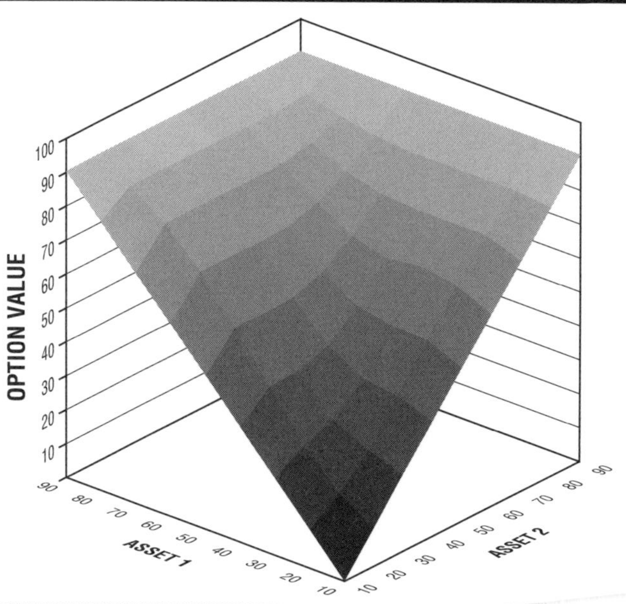

another asset but, perhaps for structural reasons, cannot. Dehnad, however, says he has seen an uptick in interest from customers, particularly corporates and financial institutions, who have LIBOR-based liabilities and Prime-based assets and want to preserve their current profit based on this spread by buying a put, i.e. a floor, based on the spread between Prime and LIBOR.

Pricing some of the simplier rainbow options, such as the outfperformance option for two assets, actually only depends effectively on one asset even though they superficially seem to depend on two.

Buying a put or floor on the difference between Prime and LIBOR is an example of a spread option which is one of four basic types of rainbow options, Tatevossian explains. The other three types are based on the maximum, the minimum and the sum of two assets in most cases. The maximum allows an investor a payoff based on the better of two assets, the minimum allows for a payoff based on the worst of two assets and the sum for a payoff based on the value of a portfolio of two assets (or indices).

Derman offers the hypothetical example of a call on the maximum, or better performance, of IBM and Compaq stock where the strike price is 100. If at the call's expiration IBM has moved from 100 to 110 and Compaq to 108, the maximum of 110 and 108 is 110. Since the strike is 100, the call pays out $10. Tatevossian explains that the option to obtain the better of two assets can be regarded as a position in one of the assets combined with an option to exchange it for the other asset. Dehnad, on the other hand, offers a formulaic representation of a call on the maximum of two assets: max [0, max (S1, S2)-X], where S1 is the price of asset 1 and S2 is the price of asset 2 and X is the strike.

Pricing some of the simpler rainbow options, such as the outperformance option for two assets, actually only depends effectively on one asset even though they superficially seem to depend on two, says Derman. The options' value can be arrived at by standard Black-Scholes, binomial tree or American-style option pricing techniques. Says Derman, "Rainbow options that truly depend on more than one factor, such as the option of the maximum of two stocks [see graph], can be solved with multi-factor pricing models requiring, for example, trinomial or quadrinomial trees or Monte Carlo simulation techniques for European-style options."

In using the Margrabe pricing model, Tatevossian notes that the pricing variables include the volatility of both assets, the correlation coefficient between the assets (which is based on the trader's assumptions), the dividend yield or pay out of each asset and the volatility of the ratio of the assets.

COMMODITY CURVES

Commodity futures curves indicate the prices for the forward delivery and payment of underlying commodities. Positive commodity curves are known as contango markets, while negative curves are known as backwardation markets. Contango curves are generally found in weaker commodity markets where there is sufficient availability of the underlying, says Louise Rowsell, associate director-commodity derivatives at Mitsubishi Finance International. Backwardation markets exist where there is an actual or perceived lack of supply, she explains.

Historically, industrial and soft commodities have exhibited both positive and negative forward curves. Gold markets rarely if ever exhibit an inverted curve, says Rowsell. As far as the consumer is concerned, the supplies of gold for industrial purposes is sufficient to meet any demand. This is because, historically, gold has been used as a store of value, kept in vaults by central banks to support their currencies, she continues.

Markets are propelled into backwardation by actual or expected short-term lack of supply. In these instances the buyer is prepared to pay a premium for near-term availability. The term coined for this premium is 'convenience yield', explains Rowsell. The convenience yield is measured between adjacent delivery months and exhibits a strong term structure where, when problems arise, prices show an exponential increase towards the shortest-term delivery, she says. In an arbitrage-free environment, the price difference between the asset at spot and at a given point in the future should be equal to the financing and storage of the asset for that period.

Commodity derivatives are explicitly dependent on a variety of factors including storage, supply and production, explains Emmanuel Pfeffer, v.p. and head of energy derivatives at Société Générale in Paris. Fundamentally, as in any other market, commodity prices are driven by supply and demand balances. However, in times of actual or perceived lack of supply, prices

DOLLAR & YEN WTI CURVES

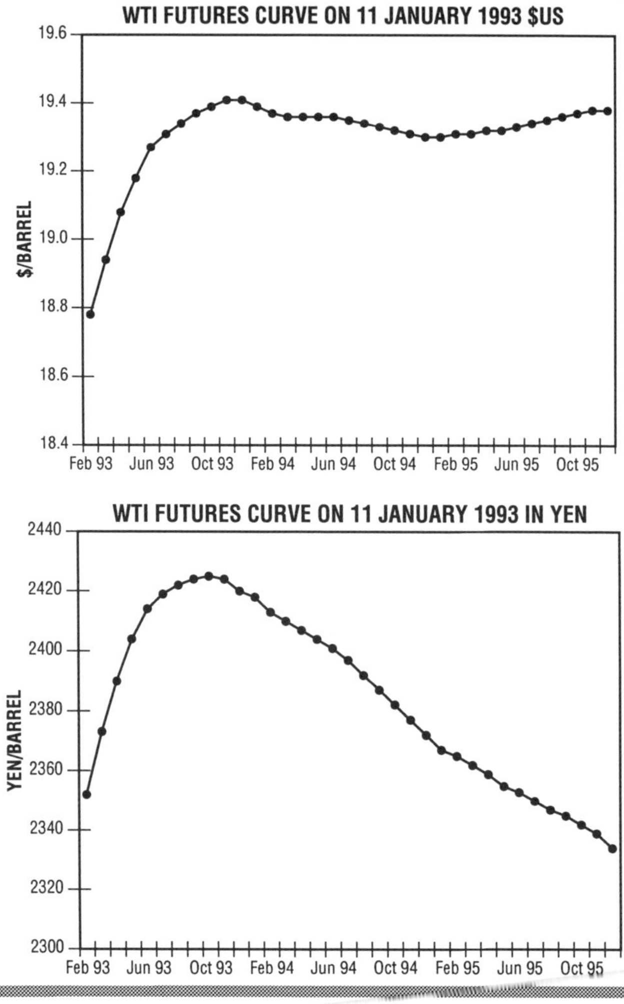

across the curve will be supported, or indeed rise, while the short end of the curve will be driven higher by consumers willing to pay premium for availability, Rowsell explains. Consequently, prices for shorter-term delivery are more volatile than prices for longer-term delivery, she says.

The pricing of commodity curves is conditional on the futures markets for the near six-eight months from spot, says Andy Gooch, commodity derivatives trader at Crédit Lyonnais Rouse Derivatives in London. Further out on the curve, liquidity and breadth is lacking on the commodity exchanges and so curves reflect market-makers' expectations to a greater degree. The lack of liquidity at the long end of the curve also presents traders with greater curve risk than that found in other derivative sectors, says Gooch. Many firms are conducting research on playing the commodity curve, according to Pfeffer. But arbitrage plays on a curve are limited.

> Historically, industrial and soft commodities have exhibited both positive and negative forward curves... Many firms are conducting research on playing the commodity curve.

The base currency of virtually all traded commodities is the U.S. dollar. For non-U.S. companies with future commodity assets and liabilities, the dollar cash flow must be translated into the domestic currency, notes Rowsell. The calculation of the forward foreign exchange curves is based on the interest rate differential between currencies. This translation may dramatically change the shape of that forward commodity curve.

Mitsubishi has structured oil-linked bonds in order to take advantage of the spot and forward values of both currency and commodity prices, says Rowsell. One example was a bond in yen to capitalize on the difference between the yen-denominated WTI curve compared to the dollar-denominated curve (see graphs), according to Rowsell. In the example, because of the strong yen, oil was 15% cheaper in yen than the average price of the past eight years for

Japanese users. The five-year forward oil price in the example implies a spot price of $18 if adjusted for inflation at 3%, says Rowsell. Mitsubishi linked redemption of the bond to the spot value of oil in yen, allowing Japanese fund managers to take advantage of the window of opportunity, says Rowsell.

INDEX AMORTIZING NOTES AND SWAPS

Index amortizing notes and swaps are amortizing structures whose rate of amortization is based on the changes of a specific index. Index amortizing notes and swaps are usually indexed to LIBOR or the yield of the constant maturity Treasuries (CMTs), notes Kosrow Dehnad, v.p. in charge of new product development at Chase Securities in New York.

Index amortizing notes and swaps are more than two years old. Daniel Seymour, sr. associate-global swaps and options at Barclays Bank in New York, estimates that a notional amount reaching into the tens of billions of dollars has been invested in index amortizing swaps. Dehnad says they have attracted investors who, in light of steep yield curves and high volatility, attempt to obtain a yield pickup. They have been popular with regional banks and other natural holders of mortgage-backed securities.

One reason for their popularity is that the structures have return characteristics that replicate MBS, such as collateralized mortgage obligations. Typically their weighted-average life (average maturity) shortens when rates drop and extends when they rise, while Seymour adds that index amortizing notes specifically allow investors to choose the index and provide for a quantifiable prepayment schedule as well as flexibility in the choice of coupon payments.

The prepayment schedule is derived from an amortization table that is constructed prior to the buying of the note or entering into the swap. The table relates various changes in the index to the amount amortized for a given coupon period. It also shows shortening (i.e. prepayment) and extension risks associated with the index amortizing note. These risks are reduced by two important features of the index amortizing notes and swaps: the lockout period, which provides investor protection against prepayment during the early life of the structure, and the final maturity, the point by which all interest and principal payments will be paid. The key to these features is that their length can be customized to meet investors' needs and risk appetite.

An index amortizing swap—Dehnad calls it an index principal swap—behaves like an index amortizing note in terms of its payoff. The difference is that the note is an on-balance sheet transaction while the swap is transacted off-balance sheet, according to Dehnad. Peter Decrem, v.p. at Salomon Brothers in New York, notes more importantly that in a stable rate environment index

PERFORMANCE OF AN INDEX PRINCIPAL SWAP VS. A REGULAR SWAP

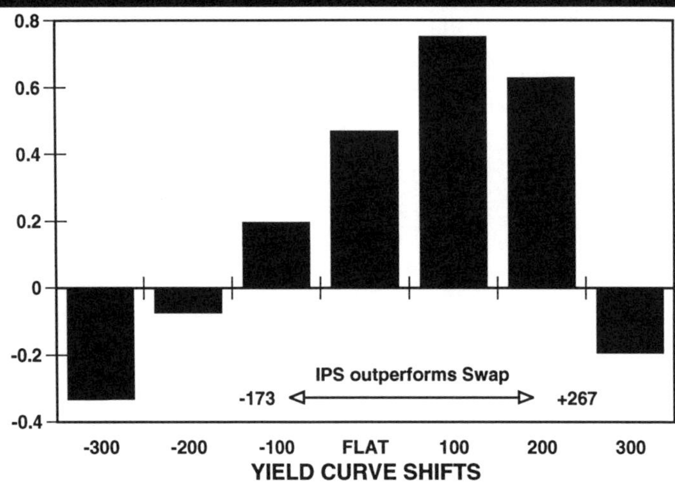

Source: Deutsche Bank Financial Products

principal swaps outperform regular swaps and underperform them in an unstable environment (see graph). Dehnad adds that hedging index principal swaps is an art and depends on interest rates, the lockout period and the dealer's risk appetite in the use of Eurofutures, Treasuries and options.

> Index amortizing notes specifically allow investors to choose the index and provide for a quantifiable prepayment schedule...

For example, consider a mock index principal swap where an investor receives a fixed rate of 5.29% on a notional amount of $100 million and pays the three-month LIBOR with a two-year lockout and a five-year maturity. If LIBOR is above 5% the swap does not amortize, but does so completely if it falls below 3%—given that amortization is based on a linear (or continuous) interpolation for a LIBOR setting between 5% and 3%. If after the two-year lockout LIBOR moves to 4%, the notional amount until the next reset is $50 million (it amortizes by 50%), which is a linear interpolation between zero amortization at 5% or higher LIBOR and complete amortization at 3% or less LIBOR.

In other words, says Dehnad, since 4% LIBOR is halfway between 3% and 5%, the swap amortizes at 50%. But if at the next resetting LIBOR is at 4.5%, the notional amount is further reduced by 25% (or to $37.5 million). Additionally, there is a cleanup level such that if the swap's notional amount falls below $5 million, for instance, the swap completely amortizes.

All instruments sharing returns similar to MBS have negative convexity, notes Decrem. "The price of a negatively convex bond does not increase at the same rate (in a falling rate environment) as it declines (in a rising rate environment)," he says. "This results from the investor having implicitly sold the dealer an option to call away the bond or swap."

SMILES AND FROWNS

Smiles and frowns are the expressions given to the shape of implied volatility curves when looking at a two dimensional graph of volatility and strike, or the shape of volatility surfaces when one looks at a graph of volatility, strike and time. Smiles and frowns are also known as skews.

As its name suggests, a smile is a U-shaped curve taking the at-the-money strike as the mid-point, with the implied volatility increasing to left and right for the out-of-the money calls and puts respectively, says Mike Greene, manager of new products at Royal Bank of Canada in London. A frown is the opposite of this phenomenon, he continues.

The expressions have been in the market for 3-4 years, says Greene. As the options markets have matured and gained greater liquidity, so the phenomena of smiles and frowns have become more easily discernible, he continues. In illiquid markets they can still be seen if one takes the mid-market levels (i.e. the mid-point between the bid/offer spreads for an option's volatility) but wider spreads have tended to hide their presence, he says.

Smiles and frowns are purely a reflection of market data and there is no formula to determine the shape of the volatility curve, says Marc Lansonneur, risk manager at Société Générale in London. The curve which one would most commonly expect to see for options would be a smile, says Greene. This in turn is a reflection of the pragmatic principle that institutions do not want to sell options for nothing, even if an option may have little chance of reaching an out-of-the money strike level, says Edward Charles, v.p.-investor derivative marketing at J.P. Morgan in London.

Sophisticated interbank players and corporates make plays on smiles and frowns when they see the opportunity to take volatility premium, according to Greene. There are two basic strategies investors can use to take advantage of the shape of the volatility surface, says Charles. If the volatility curve is U-shaped premium can be generated by selling out-of-the-money options, while players can take advantage of a frown-shaped curve by buying out-of-the-money options.

In a curve environment with no skew the most effective strategy would be to buy out-of-the money options and sell an at-the-money straddle, says Lansonneur. This strategy would limit any possible losses and provide potential upside, he said. But in a flat curve environment banks' pricing models will cause them to add a spread to the volatility rather than selling an option at a very low price. This can create a skew, so lessening the chances of a no-skew play, and protecting institutions from being long premium, Lansonneur explains.

One of the major reasons that a smile effect can be seen in the

VOLATILITIES FOR 3-MONTH US$/YEN OPTIONS

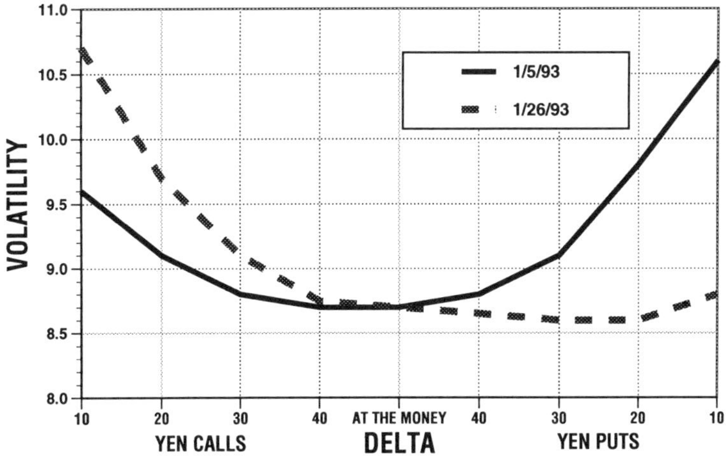

Source: *Royal Bank of Canada*

markets is out-of-the-money options offer corporates a cheap way of buying options. The more players who are prepared to buy these options the greater the volatility premium will be, Greene says. Out-of-the money options will have a low premium because they have less time value, says Lansonneur.

> If the volatility curve is U-shaped premium can be generated by selling out-of-the-money options, while players can take advantage of a frown-shaped curve by buying out-of-the-money options.

Market pressures and expectations are also major factors in driving the shape of the curve, says Greene. This in turn means that a curve may not be a straight smile or frown but can exhibit a lopsided grin. For example, on January 5, 1993, the market felt that US$/yen was likely to move higher, and potentially sharply higher, so resulting in higher volatilities. As a result, low delta yen puts were being sold at a large premium. On the other hand the premium and volatilities for yen calls were much lower as it was felt that any fall in US$/yen would be slow. The volatility curve for that date exhibits a lopsided grin which is more positive on the puts side (see graph).

On January 26 the situation had reversed, Greene explains. There was an expectation of a sharp fall in $/yen rates which would lead to higher volatilities, so there is a dramatic smile on the yen call side of the curve. Japanese exporters were known to be looking to sell the dollar if the currency moved higher, so limiting upside potential, he continued. As a result there is a small frown effect on the yen put side where out-of-the-money options (down to 20-delta) are at a discount, he explains.

The increase in more exotic products, in particular path-dependent options, means that more sophisticated means of arriving at the volatility smile curve for options will have to be worked on, says Greene. This is because volatility curves can fundamentally affect the way path-dependent options—such as knock outs—are priced and hedged, he continues.

MONTE CARLO SIMULATIONS

Monte Carlo Simulations involve long ago discovered principles of uncertainty, but since the mid to late 1970s have been used to price financial products such as derivatives. Kosrow Dehnad, v.p. in charge of new product development at Chase Securities in New York, notes that "simulation is a controlled statistical sampling that generates possible realizations of a system (e.g., possible barrier option values) using appropriate probability distributions and their relationships." Regarding MCS specifically, John Hull, professor-faculty of management at the University of Toronto and principal at A-J Financial Systems, says it involves using random numbers to sample many different paths that the underlying security could follow in a risk-neutral world.

Dehnad notes that by using random numbers one can generate, for example, possible paths that three-month LIBOR can take every three months for the next two years, given the term structure of interest rates, volatility and certain distribution assumptions (see graph). Nowadays the random numbers are generated using high speed computers that used the "mixed congruential method." Dehnad explains, however, that even though numbers so generated pass statistical tests for randomness, they are in fact pseudorandom because the formula renders the sequence of such numbers predictable.

Random numbers are used to create possible price paths for assets whose terminal value determines an option's payoff. Regarding, for example, an option whose payoff depends on two assets, Armand Tatevossian, director-financial products group at

Barclays de Zoete Wedd in New York, notes that each assets' paths must be sampled on each simulation run and the option's terminal value is calculated based on each run. The results are then averaged for all simulation runs—as many as 10,000—thus allowing for the current option value.

He offers the example of an option on the Nikkei 225 index's value paid in U.S. dollars. "The option's payout at expiration depends on the Nikkei 225's value and the U.S. dollar/yen exchange rate," he notes. "In modelling this option using MCS, a simulated price path for the Nikkei index is constructed along with a correlated price path for the dollar/yen exchange rate. The two paths comprise a single simulation run, from which the option's terminal value is calculated. The arithmetic average of a large number of simulation runs, discounted back to the present, provides an estimate of the option's current value."

Mark Garman, finance professor at the University of California, Berkeley and principal at Financial Engineering Associates, a maker of Monte Carlo simulation software, notes that MCS finds its origin

MONTE CARLO OUTPUT REALIZATIONS
Three Month LIBOR, Two Years from Spot

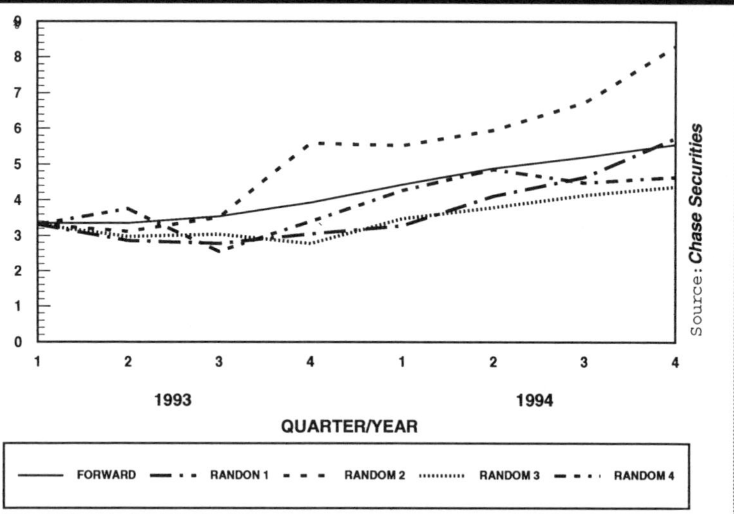

with Karl Pearson, a statistician. In 1892, Pearson went to Monte Carlo for two weeks and his observations regarding a dishonest gambling wheel led to his publishing his probability theory in 1900. The theory's link to finance is University of Waterloo finance professor Phelim Boyle, who published in 1977 an article called "Options: A Monte Carlo Approach" in the Journal of Financial Economics.

In 1892, statistician Karl Pearson went to Monte Carlo for two weeks and his observations regarding a dishonest gambling wheel led to his publishing his probability theory in 1900.

In 1979, Mark Rubinstein, John Cox and Stephen Ross (along with William Sharpe) created the binomial tree method, says Garman and Tatevossian. This method shows possible future option price distributions given the underlying's price moves using binomial distribution to build a probability tree. Indeed, some option pricing models use a binomial tree as the underlying framework upon which a Monte Carlo-style run is carried out (e.g., lookback options), says Tatevossian.

Both Garman and Hull note that MCS is better used to price European-style rather than American-style options because MCS, says Hull, "works forward from the beginning to the end of the life of a security" and can thus handle the complex payoffs associated with exotic barrier, compound, average rate and contingent options. "Decision-dependent problems," which favor American options, move backward in time and are more conducive to the binomial tree method, Garman explains. Also, compared to the binomial tree method, MCS is more efficient as the number of underlying variables increase, Hull says.

Tatevossian notes that one of the first widespread uses of MCS was in determining the fair price, option-adjusted spread and effective duration of mortgage-backed securities. He adds it is now used to value index amortizing swaps, forward "reset" floating rate notes, periodic "capped" swaps, as well as swap credit risk. MCS is also used to measure the performance of various option hedging schemes, such as "hedging through the cap (strike)" and dynamic hedging.

Of late there has been renewed concern that the random numbers in MCS may not be random because at some point past a billion or so simulations random numbers repeat themselves. But, Garman, Hull and Dehnad say variance reduction techniques such as the use of antithetic variables and control variates reduce the number of simulation runs and errors, as well the simulation time.

TERM STRUCTURE OF VOLATILITY

The term structure of volatility is the different implied volatilities for options of different terms (maturities). Fundamental to an understanding of term structure of volatility is the principle of mean reversion, which suggests that over the long term the market expects volatility to revert to a mean value or norm.

The volatility of a three-month option, for example, reflects market perceptions of the average volatility for that period. If one-month volatility is lower than normal, three-month volatility is likely to be higher because the market expects volatility to return to normal levels, reverting back to the mean. Short-term options exhibit greater volatility than longer-term options because the latter are based on an average gleaned from more data over a longer period, causing the term structure of volatility to smooth out towards the longer end when represented by a curve, and to show greater variance at the shorter end (see graph). The effects of smiles and frowns are more pronounced in the near months for the Nikkei options than in the longer term, according to Les Clewlow, research fellow-Financial Options Research Centre at the Warwick Business School.

Smiles and frowns can be seen in the Nikkei options closest to maturity as this marks the crucial period when option sellers must address their hedging needs, Clewlow continues. The biases disappear quickly as traders' hedging worries decrease, he continues. This leads to volatility smoothing out for all the Nikkei options as their maturities increase. The smoothing effect is also created by liquidity being distributed more evenly between all the strikes, he continues.

The principle of mean reversion is common to the term structure of both interest rates and volatility and tends to limit the application of the Black Scholes model for interest rate options as it will look at the underlying interest rates in terms of random motion. In theory this would mean that interest rates could fluctuate between zero and infinity at the long end of the curve.

Though randomness appears to hold true if one looks at the interest rates of currencies over a short time frame, it becomes evident that over the longer term interest rates do move less dramatically, keeping within certain bands. Traders have to lower volatilities in their models at the longer end to take account of this fact, so creating a downward slope of the term structure curve.

The term structure of volatility is used by up to 80% of currency derivative traders, who can employ it for speculative purposes, estimates David Denora, v.p.-head of currency options at Union Bank of Switzerland in London. It is particularly useful for calen-

IMPLIED VOLATILITY OF NIKKEI OPTIONS

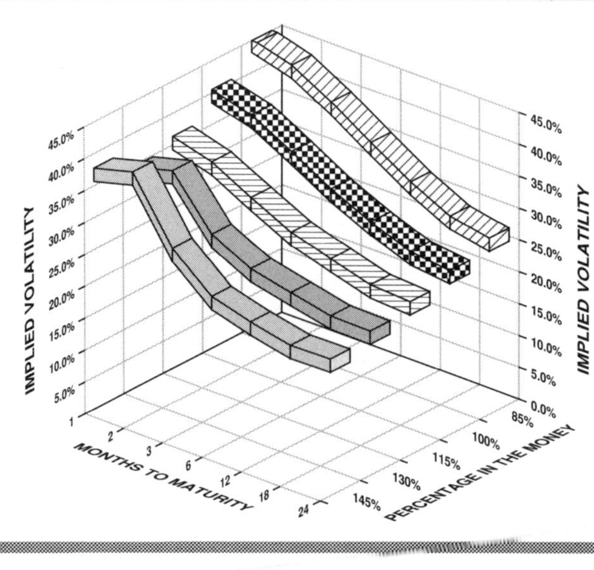

dar spread plays, where an option which has been written expires before an option which has been purchased.

Traders are faced with difficulties when looking for volatility arbitrage possibilities in interest rate products such as caps, floors and swaptions. For example, a trader looking for arbitrage possibilities between one- and two-year caps on a three-month interest rate is dealing with two different products because they are options on different underlying forward rate agreements. To determine arbitrage possibilities the trader will have to determine a forward volatility rate, but that will depend on his assumptions about the relative volatilities between the one- and two-year interest rates over the first year.

> Though randomness appears to hold true if one looks at the interest rates of currencies over a short time frame, it becomes evident that over the longer term interest rates do move less dramatically, keeping within certain bands.

The ability to arbitrage in fixed-income products will depend on a trader's own experience of the markets as there is no empirical data on which he can rely. There is no forward market in volatilities as there is for interest rates. Tradeable sets of options with different maturities but the same underlying interest rate do not exist and so there are no methods to lock in profits.

Using certain assumptions a term structure model for an option of a year or more can be created. For instance, a model could assume that spot volatility—volatility of a one-day option—varies in a certain way over time. Following that, patterns and assumptions based on past currency option volatility can be fed into the model and used to derive an entire term structure from the spot implied volatility.

PERIODIC CAPS

A periodic interest rate cap—whether standing alone or embedded in a structured floating rate note—is a sequence of "caplets" in which the individual strikes depend on future values of LIBOR and are therefore not known in advance, according to Leon Tatevossian, v.p.-derivatives research at Salomon Brothers in New York. Kosrow Dehnad, v.p. in charge of new product development at Chase Securities in New York, describes the strike of the periodic cap with the formula: minimum (LIBOR, previous strike) + pre-specified spread. Tatevossian adds that if a floating rate note has an embedded periodic cap, then the current coupon and the strike of the next applicable option are determined at each reset date.

Because a periodic cap's strike changes as LIBOR changes, the payoff in the transaction depends on the path of LIBOR and the cap is therefore regarded as a path-dependent option, note both Dehnad and John Paganucci, associate-index principal swaps at BT Securities. In this regard, the periodic cap differs from the regular cap where the strike is known at origination.

Paganucci illustrates one of the differences by detailing the behavior of a periodic cap and a regular cap (in this case a step-up strike cap). He says a periodic cap-based swap provides the seller with a net carry (the difference between what the seller receives and pays) that is greater than the swap that uses a step-up cap. Dehnad defines a step-up cap as one whose strike goes up for subsequent periods at predetermined levels (see graph).

Paganucci notes that both trades—which are extrapolated from the implied forward rate—have four-year tenors, begin March 1993 and reset quarterly. With the embedded periodic cap, the seller receives three-month LIBOR, which cannot increase more than 25 basis points per quarter, plus a compensatory spread. The step-up strike cap seller receives LIBOR plus a smaller spread with a cap strike which increases by 25 basis points per reset from the implied forward LIBOR. With the step-up strike cap, all the strikes are defined on the trade date.

Like Dehnad, Paganucci explains that "it's an optimal time for trades to be put on due to record high volatility and unprecedented steepness of the yield curve." He adds that the periodic caps have recently been particularly attractive among a variety of cap sellers—from corporates to money managers to pension funds—and estimates that they have so far generated about $10 billion in activity.

Periodic caps are preferred by investors because, unlike step-up strike caps, a steep yield curve increases their value rather than the overall level of rates. Paganucci explains that sellers "believe the yield curve is too steep and that rates will not actually increase by the pace implied," the point being that rates that rise too rapidly will trigger the cap and create a loss for the option seller. Tatevossian concurs, referring to this loss as the "lag effect." He adds that, with a periodically capped floater, increases in the note's

CUSTOMER'S NET CARRY

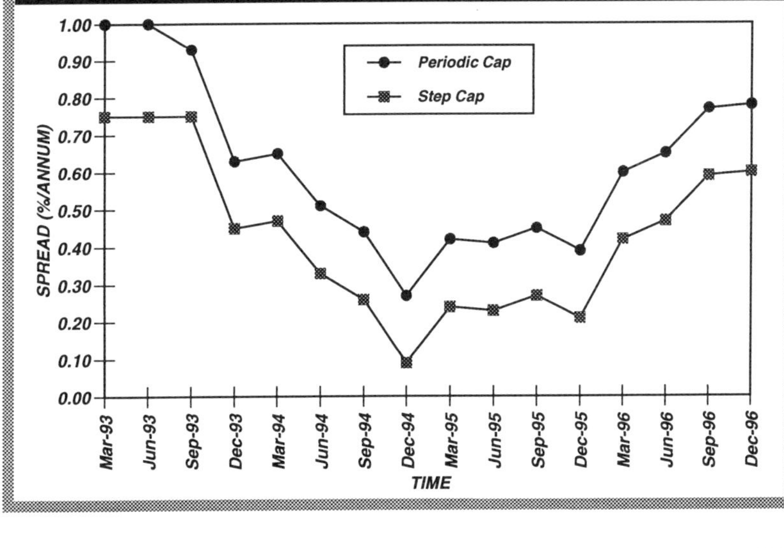

coupon can lag increases in the interest rate index.

Paganucci contends that periodic caps were born about six months ago at Bankers Trust and were originally used in "one-way floaters"—which are FRNs combined with the sale of a periodic cap and the purchase of a floor to insure that the coupon never falls below the previous coupon. Armand Tatevossian, director-global swaps and options group at Barclays de Zoete Wedd in New York, adds that last summer Merrill Lynch placed one-way floaters with private investors and referred to the embedded option as a "variable strike cap."

> A periodic cap's strike changes as LIBOR changes and is therefore regraded as a path-dependent option.

Cap dealers like to buy periodic caps from issuers and swap counterparties because the dealers are buying caps at attractive volatility levels with implied strikes that are close to an at-the-money-forward, says Barclays' Tatevossian. He adds that the market risk with one-way floaters is that the embedded option may cause the note to underperform conventional FRNs when interest rates rise rapidly, the curve steepens or volatility increases. Tatevossian also notes that many borrowers who have issued one-way floaters have swapped into LIBOR at levels below their normal funding costs. He adds that asset managers have combined LIBOR-based investments with periodic cap-based swaps to enhance returns on their money market securities.

One-way floaters, or periodic caps, are priced using Monte Carlo Simulations. Dehnad notes that the seller's spread is a function of the cap's value. He adds that periodic caps are hedged using Eurodollar futures and swaps and explains that care must be taken with gamma risk. Says Dehnad, "In hedging, one looks at the structure's sensitivity to a small movement in the price of the underlying instruments used to generate the yield curve (e.g., Eurofutures), and then decides how many of these instruments are needed to make the position delta-neutral with respect to the above movements.

PUT-CALL PARITY

Put-call parity is the relationship which rules out the possibility of arbitrage between European puts and calls with the same strike and underlying. Given similar market conditions and, most importantly, similar volatility levels, put-call parity will allow the value of European-style calls to be determined from the value of European-style puts, or vice versa, according to Neil Dodgson, associate director-interest rate risk management at NatWest Capital Markets.

The relationship is clearly visible diagrammatically (see graph), according to Dodgson. The payoff from the DM forward rate agreement (FRA) which begins in three months and expires in six months with a 7.30% strike should equal the payoff from buying a cap and selling a floor of similar strikes and maturities, he explains. The sum of the two options is identical to purchasing the forward rate agreement, he notes.

If the option is an at-the-money forward, (i.e. the forward rate equals the strike price) then the cap will have the same value as the floor, assuming that the volatility is equal for the two options, Dodgson explains. The put-call parity for caps and floor can be expressed as:

cap = floor + discounted value of (forward rate - strike)

The same relationship can be expressed for European-style options on non-dividend-paying equities, says Kosrow Dehnad, v.p. in charge of new product development at Chase Securities. The equity call should be equal to the put plus the price of the equity minus the present value of borrowing the strike.

Put-call parity provides a basis for creating synthetic option positions using puts, calls and the underlying in tandem, according to Richard Leighton, manager-currency and option derivatives at Midland Global Markets. For example, if a corporation goes long an at-the-money U.S. dollar call option with a strike of $1.63, and short a put option with the same strike, the net effect is one of buying dollars forward at a price of $1.63, Leighton explains. The reverse strategy can be used to short the forward. If the values of two of the elements in the put-call parity relationship are known, the third unknown can be attained, he continues.

If put-call parity breaks down, investors can create a synthetic option to replicate the action of an option more cheaply. For instance, a corporate may wish to purchase an out-of-the-money U.S. dollar put with a low delta and a strike of $1.50 because it expects the dollar to fall, Leighton explains. But market-makers do not like to be short low delta because of the risks involved, so volatility on the option will be marked up, he explains. Instead of purchasing the put with a volatility of 14%, the corporate

PAYOFF OF DM FRA VS. BUYING A CAP AND SELLING A FLOOR

Source: *NatWest Capital Markets*

could purchase a 90% delta call with a volatility of around 13.5%, and sell the forward to arrive at a synthetic replication of the put.

There will be a natural drive to the restoration of put-call parity as bidders hoping to exploit the arbitrage opportunity will force up the call volatility, says Dehnad. Although volatilities for puts and calls can differ, additional overhead costs will mean that prices may only differ by a small amount, therefore creating limits for put-call parity where implied volatility can be within a range, according to Les Clewlow, research fellow with the Financial Options Research Centre at the Warwick Business School.

> Put-call parity provides a basis for creating synthetic option positions using puts, calls and the underling in tandem.

Put-call parity will only hold effectively for European-style options, Clewlow says. An American call will behave as a European call (provided there is no dividend) because investors will tend to hold the option until expiration. This is because they do not wish to lose the time value of the money they would have to invest in the underlying or the insurance value of the option, according to Dehnad.

The same argument does not hold for an American-style put. An investor holding the put and the underlying stock can exercise the option and sell the stock with the time value in his favor, because he will be receiving income early which can then be invested, explains Dehnad. But the investor will lose the insurance value of the option. The decision to exercise depends on whether the loss of insurance is outweighed by gains on time value of money, he continues. Consequently, the put-call parity in the case of American-style option becomes an inequality: that is to say, an American put is at least as valuable or more valuable than a European put, and an American call has the same value as a European call, provided there is no dividend.

CORRELATION

Correlation or, more strictly, co-variance, provides a measure of the risk for a portfolio of two [or more] assets. Formally, correlation between two assets is defined as the co-variance of those two assets divided by the product of the standard deviations of each of them from their mean. According to Kosrow Dehnad, v.p. in charge of new products at Chase Securities in New York, English anthropologist/statistician Francis Galton discovered correlation around the turn of the century. In studying the height relationship between fathers and sons, Galton developed regression analysis, out of which grew the concept of correlation.

Dehnad notes that correlation also comes in different forms such as rank correlation (a measure of the co-movement of two entities using ranks), multiple correlation (a measure of the co-movement of the linear relationship between one variable and a set of other variables) and partial correlation (where the correlation between two assets is measured given the level of another variable or asset).

Correlation ranges from -1 to +1, says Gifford Fong, president of Gifford Fong Associates in California. A correlation close to zero, typically like that between equities and commodities, indicates uncorrelated risk and that assets behave independently of each other. Dehnad observes, on the other hand, that, although independence implies zero correlation, the converse is not always true. However, if the two variables are normally distributed, then zero correlation and independence are equivalent.

A positive correlation approaching +1, typically seen between a stock and the general stock market, denotes assets that track each other. Conversely, a negative correlation, for example, between money market and equity returns, indicates movement between assets such that as one falls the other rises. The impact on option pricing, in particular for exchange options, which are options to exchange one asset for another, is that they are cheaper the more positive their correlation and more expensive the more negative their correlation, according to Jason Wei, a finance professor at the University of Saskatchewan in Canada.

Edgar Peters, senior manager-asset allocation at PanAgora Asset Management, links correlation to chaos theory, which says things that appear to move randomly actually move deterministically. He contends that the lognormal distribution of asset returns does not always have a bell shape and that market movements are not random, roll-of-the-dice, walks. "Correlation can change at any time without warning," he says, noting that hedges that depend on stable correlations may be stable for a while but can become unstable. Fong agrees and observes that when hedging derivatives care should be taken to determine what the true correlation will be over the hedge's life.

HISTORICAL CORRELATION BASED ON SEMI-ANNUAL RETURNS

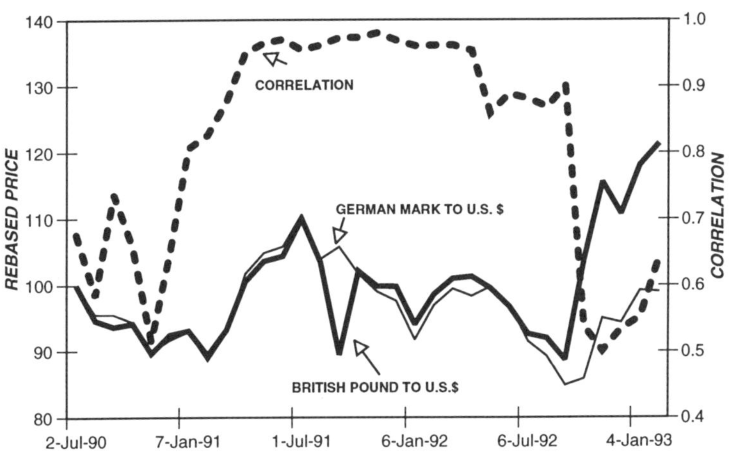

Source: *Barclays de Zoete Wedd*

Peters cites the slightly positive .55 correlation between stock and bond returns over 10 years which, when measured quarterly, every six months or yearly, exhibits a higher correlation, or even a negative one. Historical data can be a first measure of correlation which is subject to significant change given asset volatility. From late 1990 to October 1992, when the pound traded within bands set by the European Exchange Rate Mechanism, the DM/£ correlation was high but dropped dramatically, nearly 0.50, after the European currency crisis (see graph). Peters, however, comments that correlation instability is less severe with derivatives.

Increased investor interest in derivatives used to switch between assets has made correlation a key element in measuring risk and pricing options on the assets.

Increased investor interest in derivatives used to switch between assets has made correlation a key element in measuring risk and pricing options on the assets. Correlation, along with the number and riskiness of the assets and time horizon, is crucial to pricing Fong's multiple-asset option, which takes the return of the best performing asset, less the predetermined strategy cost. Meanwhile, Wei has developed a closed-end pricing formula for differential swaps. He says practitioners, while somewhat familiar with exchange rate/foreign interest rate correlation, tend to ignore the correlation between domestic and foreign interest rates as significant parameters in pricing diff swaps.

William Margrabe, creator of the rainbow option pricing model and v.p.-derivatives research group/equity portfolio analysis at Salomon Brothers in New York, notes that the price of a rainbow option typically depends on one or more correlations among other assumptions, such as dividend yields, volatilities, underlying prices and, in some cases, interest rates. This opens the novel possibility of using rainbow options to trade correlation just as one would trade volatility, Margrabe says. "To trade [relatively] pure correlation, you will want to offset the sensitivity of the outperformance option to volatilities by trading ordinary options and offset its sensitivity to the underlyings by delta hedging," he adds.

FORWARD SWAPS

Forward swaps are executed now but begin at a prearranged date in the future. A plain vanilla swap becomes effective within two business days after being executed, so any swap beginning at a later date can technically be classed as a forward swap, according to Gail Benun, v.p. at Bank of America in London responsible for marketing derivative products in southern Europe.

Forward swaps allow asset and liability managers to implement their views of the yield curve, Benun explains. Corporations may wish to lock into forward rates in the belief they will be lower than the spot rate at a future date but at the same time may wish to leave their liabilities floating at an attractive lower rate for a period. In an inverted yield curve environment, a corporation may wish to lock in its rate using a forward swap, Benun explains. Municipalities have used them to lock in rates for future debt refinancings.

Forward swap rates are determined by swap yield differentials between the swap position the corporation wants to put on and the swap positions the swap house will need to enter into as a hedge, explains Benun. If, for instance, a corporation wants to enter into a swap beginning in one year's time for a duration of four years (a "one year-by-four year" or "1*4" swap), the swap house will have to enter into two offsetting swaps immediately to hedge its position (see graph).

If the end user wants to pay fixed in one year, the swap house will immediately enter into a five-year swap paying fixed and receiving floating, says Benun. Additionally, the swap house will have to enter a one-year swap receiving fixed and paying floating from spot to one year. The one-year swap offsets the cash flows on the five-year swap for the first year, while the forward four-year swap offsets the cashflows for the last four years of the five-year swap, Benun explains.

If the yield curve is upward sloping, the five-year rate paid by the swap house will be higher than the one-year rate received, creating a loss or negative carry for one year, Benun says. The swap house will calculate the present value of the loss and charge it as an annuity into the one-by-four-year forward swap. That additional amount is known as the "forward premium."

If the yield curve is inverted, the premium will be negative and the one-by-four forward swap will be lower than the current spot swap rate and possibly lower than the current LIBOR rate, says Benun. In this case, a corporation can reduce its current interest expense in addition to hedging future interest expense by entering the forward swap. The differentials between the spot hedging and forward rates are therefore calculated to see whether premium is added to or subtracted from the spot swap rate paid by the end user.

Like forward swaps, swaptions also offer end users the ability to lock into rates at a future date as they are options on forward

A FORWARD SWAP HEDGE

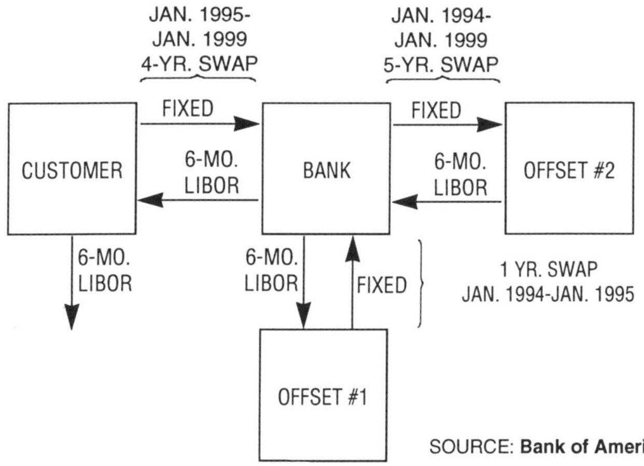

SOURCE: **Bank of America**

swaps. But forward swaps confer an obligation to enter into the swap, whereas swaptions give the end user the choice as to whether or not to lock in, says Benun. For this reason both products have different advantages for end users, explains Nick Haining, head of swap marketing at BNP Capital Markets in London.

> Forward swaps are useful for corporations with a directional view that can be improved upon by going forward on the yield curve.

Swaptions may offer solutions for corporate treasurers who are uncertain as to their cashflows and do not want to commit themselves to a forward swap, Haining says. Swaptions also provide the corporation with a product that offers protection when the interest rate environment is extremely volatile, so leaving the firm with no clear directional view, he says. If interest rates go against the corporation's position in the swaption and its predetermined view of the forward yield curve, all it will lose is the premium for the option.

Forward swaps, on the other hand, are useful for corporations with a directional view that can be improved upon by going forward on the yield curve, explains Haining. They also allow a corporation to be certain of the level of its future assets or liabilities. Forward swaps also have advantages over swaptions in that they do not require an initial outlay of premium, this being a decisive factor for companies and institutions for whom cash flows are tight, explains Haining.

Forward swaps in U.S. dollars have recently proved attractive for fund managers and cash-rich corporations because of the positive shape of the U.S. yield curve, says Haining. BNP has seen a lot of business from investors looking to pick up yield by receiving fixed, he said, though the window of opportunity may be closing as the yield curve flattens. This is resulting in a shift of interest from investors to borrowers as corporations begin to look to pay fixed, according to Haining.

STEP-UP RECOVERY FLOATERS

Step-up recovery floaters (SURFs), also known as half-CMT floaters, are floating-rate obligations that make for a relatively new yield curve play and exploit the curve's steepness. SURFs permit investors to take a combined view on the direction of rates and the shape of yield curve, riding the curve as if it were a wave.

SURFs allow issuers to provide investors with a coupon that is derived by halving the constant-maturity Treasury (CMT) rate while also paying a predetermined spread (150 basis points, for example) and providing a floor (typically 4-4.5%), according to Michael Harpe, principal in derivative products at Morgan Stanley in New York. In the case of a five-year SURF which uses a 10-year CMT rate of 7%, for example, the note's coupon would be 3.5% plus 1.50%, or 5%, with a 4.5% floor and a semi-annual coupon reset.

The CMT rate is calculated daily and published weekly by the Federal Reserve. The Fed takes the average bids on all U.S. Treasury yields for all maturities from a rotating pool of five primary dealers. Lehman Brothers, Morgan Stanley and Merrill Lynch have been among the most active dealers in SURFs. Harpe says most issues have ranged in size from $100-150 million. Timothy Skeet, senior v.p.-syndicate desk at Kidder Peabody International in London, observes that between February 18 and March 18,

1993, eight issues came to market totalling some $800 million.

Issuers in Europe in the early part of 1993 included supranationals such as the World Bank, Eurofima and Council of Europe and top quality corporates such as Toyota Motor Credit. In the U.S. the bulk of the volume was issued by U.S. government agencies such as the Federal Home Loan Banks and Federal National Mortgage Association. Sudhir Krishnamurthi, senior financial officer-financial operations department at the World Bank in Washington, D.C., contends that the World Bank's five-year $100 million SURF note (a first) was issued and immediately hedged based on an absolutely market-neutral view.

Krishnamurthi adds that the World Bank's primary concern is to reduce its all-in funding cost. In this regard he validates Skeet's contention that SURFs have provided issuers with cheap sub-LIBOR funding. Harpe adds that structurally SURFs also offer

SURF COUPON RELATIVE TO LIBOR
1/2 x 10-Year AMT = 1.50% (4.50% floor)

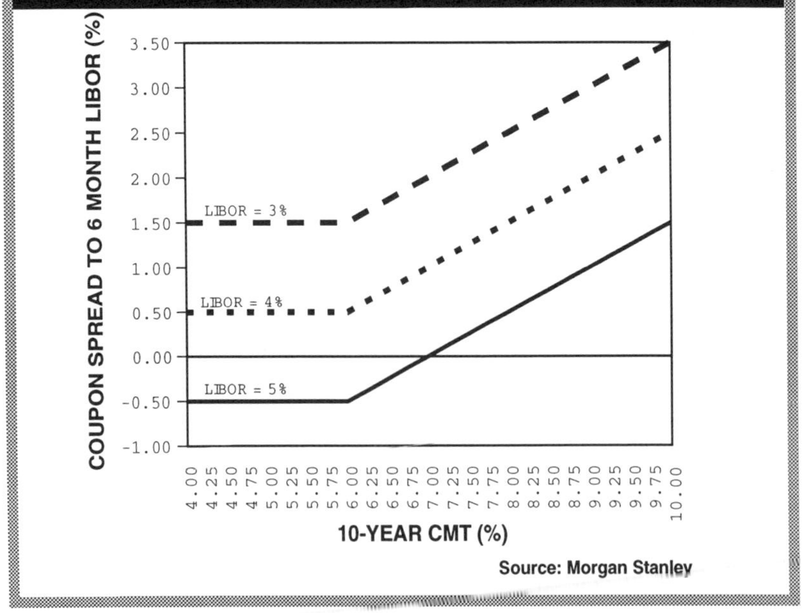

investors a great deal of flexibility in the choice of CMT and floor rates.

Skeet notes that SURFs attract investors because they provide enhanced yields in the short term.

> SURFs permit investors to take a combined view on the direction of rates and the shape of yield curve, riding the curve as if it were a wave.

Harpe says investors have included smaller financial institutions and money managers who typically buy floating rate notes, want yields that are likely to stay above LIBOR and like the SURFs' "very high floor rate." These investors are implicitly taking the view that LIBOR will remain low and the yield curve steep. At present, SURFs have higher coupons than LIBOR-based floaters. In tracking the spread between six-month LIBOR and SURFs, the latter outperforms the former when LIBOR rates are low (see graph).

SURFs would outperform fixed-rate instruments in a rising rate environment, but may underperform LIBOR-based floaters because of the deleverage feature (the 1/2 multiple). SURF's embedded floor will benefit the investor in the event of a fall in rates. In offering a higher floor, however, the issuer is compensated by offering investors a lower spread. Harpe adds further that the longer the bond's maturity the higher the spread and the floor.

Issuers can use interest rate swaps to convert the CMT-based liability into a LIBOR-based liability. In one swap the issuer pays LIBOR and receives the CMT rate minus a spread on one half of the original notional amount. In addition, the issuer does a conventional fixed-for-floating swap on one half the original notional. The dealer in the CMT-for-LIBOR swap either finds a counterparty to take the other side or dynamically hedges his exposure by managing a position in U.S. Treasury bonds or bond futures.

BOX SPREADS

The box spread is an option strategy which can offer risk-free gains and is "the Holy Grail of the derivatives world," quips Mike Hudson, chairman of the Sunrise Company in London. A box spread is created by executing vertical call and put spreads—the simultaneous purchase and sale of options with different strikes but the same expiration, according to K. Ravindran, director of global derivative product development at Toronto Dominion Bank in Toronto. Pared down to its essentials, a box spread is constructed from bear spreads and bull spreads.

A box spread will be profitable if the credit position for the strategy is greater than the difference between the strikes, explains Hudson. If the underlying stock is at 363p, the player can sell a 360 strike call at 23p and buy a 390 strike call at 10p. Simultaneously, he can buy a 360 strike put at 15p and sell a 390 strike put for 35p. The net initial credit position achieved by the strategy will be 33p, says Hudson.

If the stock is below 360p at expiration, the calls will expire worthless but both puts are in-the-money and the spread will cost 30p to close out. Above 390p the puts will be worthless, but the calls will be in the money and again the spread will cost 30p to close out.

In all the above scenarios, the sum of the intrinsic values must always equal 30p, regardless of the spot price of the stock at expiry. The player will always find that the box spread will cost 30p to close out and therefore given the initial credit of 33p the implied profit from the spread will be 3p (see graph), plus any financing advantage gained from investing the initial credit.

Conversely, one can have a net initial debit position from a box spread strategy, according to Michael Schwartz, senior v.p. and chief options strategist at Oppenheimer & Co. in New York. If the S&P 500 were at 384, a player may buy 100 in-the-money 360 strike calls for $335,000 and sell 100 calls with a strike of 410 for $42,500. Simultaneously, the player may buy 100 puts with a strike of 410 for $262,500 and sell an equal number of 360 strike puts at $65,000. This box spread would result in a debit position of $490,000. The box spread player will still achieve a gain from a net initial debit position as long as the two spreads in the strategy can be purchased for less than the difference between the strike price of the spreads, he says.

As box spreads contain debit and credit spreads, any player with a greater debit than credit is effectively lending money to the market maker, says Schwartz. Box spreads have been used in this way by market makers to finance their positions more cheaply than by borrowing from money clearing houses, he says. This is particularly true in high interest rate environments, he continues.

A BOX SPREAD

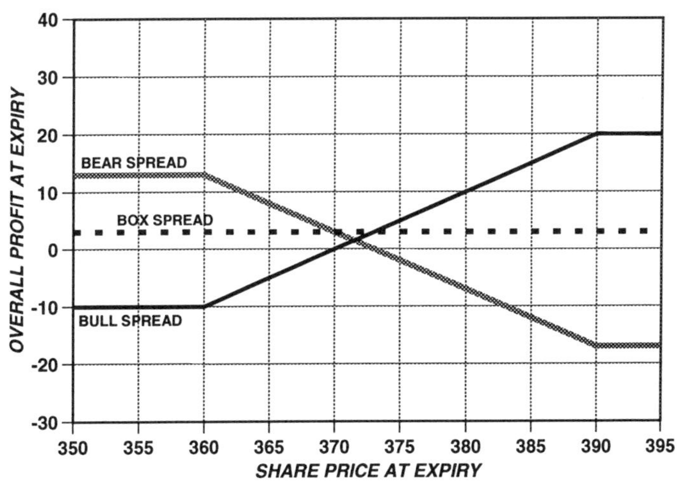

Source: ***Sunrise Co.***

U.S. corporates look to apply the box-spread strategy if they have large loss carryforwards (which they have five years to write off) and an availability of funds, according to Kevin Murphy, v.p.-retail options department at Lehman Brothers in New York. The trade offers risk-free capital gains which can be used against the loss carryforward. And box spreads can offer better after-tax returns than other taxable financial instruments, he says.

The box spread is "the Holy Grail of the derivatives world."

To make the trade worthwhile a large capital outlay will be needed to pick up the small basis points gain in a box spread, Murphy continues. A $250,000 notional box spread, for example, may only allow returns of $3,000. As a risk-free return the box spread will move with other risk-free rates. In fact, the box spread is sometimes quoted in terms of yield compared to Treasury bills, says Murphy.

Because box spreads can tie up large amounts of capital for a very small capital gain, they are not as attractive to individual investors, Murphy says. Individual investors are also not concerned by carryforwards because, unlike corporates, they have no deadline in which to offset their losses.

The other restraining factor is the "cost of carry" in the trade, explains Ravindran. Commissions and interest rates will have to be taken into account, reducing the arbitrage opportunity in the trade, he says. The strategy itself is most likely to be executed using exchange-traded contracts because they offer greater liquidity than over-the-counter products. If American-style options are used in this strategy, there is a threat of early assignment, says Hudson.

HEDGE RATIOS

Hedge ratios reveal the core relationship between a derivative product and its underlying instrument and how one mitigates the risk of the other. William Margrabe, creator of the outperformance option pricing model and v.p.-derivatives research group at Salomon Brothers in New York, says hedge ratios refer to "the number of units that one goes short (or long) an underlying instrument in order to offset the risk of owning (or shorting) a derivative product."

Armen Avanessians, v.p. in charge of currency and commodity strategies at Goldman Sachs in New York, notes that with options the hedge ratio is commonly referred to as the delta—a fractional change in an option's price corresponding to a one-point change in the underlying's price. The ratio derived from this relationship determines how much of one instrument one needs to hedge another instrument. Says Margrabe, "The hedge ratio will equal the number of units of the underlying instrument in the derivative product's replicating portfolio."

By replicating portfolio Margrabe means the portfolio of underlying instruments that behaves like the derivative product, at least for small changes in the underlying prices. "For example," Margrabe says, "in a perfect market the replicating portfolio for an at-the-money European call on the S&P 500 consists of a long position of about half a unit of the S&P 500 index portfolio (so the hedge ratio is about 1/2) and a short position in a zero-coupon bond maturing at the expiration date. The zero is worth slightly less than the S&P position, and the net value of the long and short positions equals the option premium."

The same hedging principle applies to fixed-income derivatives.

Kosrow Dehnad, v.p. in charge of new products at Chase Securities in New York, notes that Treasury bond futures can be used to hedge small parallel shifts in the yield curve in what he calls a "duration-based hedge." In this case, the hedge ratio is "equal to the value of the fixed-income asset that one is hedging times its duration divided by the value of the futures contract times the duration of the cheapest-to-deliver bond," Dehnad said.

Dehnad cites an investor who hedges a $10 million portfolio of fixed-income instruments with a duration of 8.3 years, while the Treasury bond future is trading at 109 7/32 (or 109.21875), and the cheapest-to-deliver bond has a duration of 7.2 years. Here, the hedge ratio is the number of futures contracts an investor should sell so that changes in the portfolio's value due to small yield curve shifts are offset with the gains or losses in the Treasury bond futures. In this case, the hedge ratio is $10 million times 8.3 divided by [109.21875 times 1,000 (the value of a futures contract)

HEDGE RATIO
DM Forward & Future

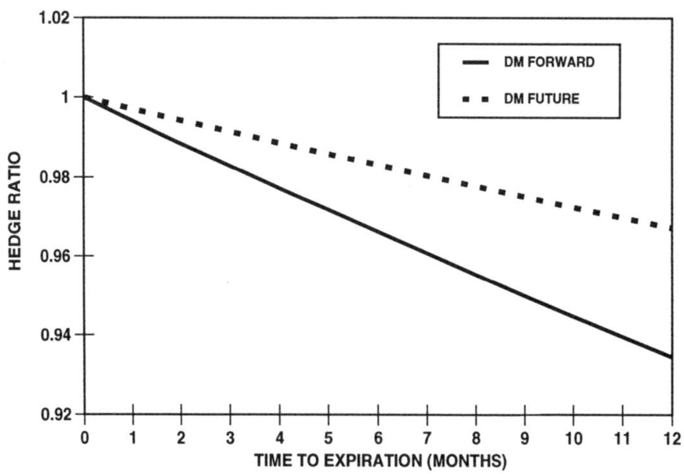

Assumes: DM rates 7.0% simple. USD rates 3.5% simple. The hedge ratio for a DM forward is given by: Present Value of 1 DM = 1/(1+DM rate * time). The hedge ratio for a DM future is given by: Present Value of 1 DM/Present Value of 1 USD = (1+USD rate *time)/(1+DM rate *time)
Source: ***Goldman Sachs***

times 7.2 (the duration of the cheapest to deliver bond)]. This ratio is equal to 105.5476, which, when rounded, equals 105 futures contracts.

Dehnad also says a hedge ratio is calculated when stock index futures are used to hedge the market risk of a portfolio of equities. The hedge ratio depends on the portfolio's beta, which essentially measures the degree of co-movement between the portfolio's value and the value of the "market portfolio," says Dehnad. He notes, "The proper number of stock index futures [the hedge ratio] needed to be sold to hedge away the market risk of this portfolio is equal to the beta times the portfolio's value divided by the futures contract's value."

> "The hedge ratio will equal the number of units of the underlying instrument in the derivative product's replicating portfolio."

For example, suppose an investor owns a $5 million equity portfolio with a beta of 1.4 and the S&P 500 index is at 400. The hedge ratio equals $5 million times 1.4 divided by [400 times $500 (the dollar value of each S&P 500 futures contract)]. The ratio in this case is equal to 35 contracts—the number of contracts the investor needs to sell to hedge the portfolio's market risk.

Avanessians says hedge ratios also hedge currency risk by using the spot market. For instance, if an investor expects a large Deutsche mark cash inflow one year from now, he could hedge by selling a DM forward or future to lock in today's rate a year ahead of time. To arrive at the present value of one DM a year from now, as well as to know how much spot (or cash) to sell, divide one by 1.07, for a hedge ratio of 0.934, or the amount of spot needed to hedge one DM forward contract (see graph). The formula assumes an interest rate of 0.07%, which is multiplied by time in years (in this case, 1 year or 12 months). One can also use spot to hedge a DM futures position using the formula given in the graph.

Finally, Margrabe notes that hedging costs determine the price of a derivative product offered by a dealer. "If you can hedge it, you can price it," he says, adding, "If you know the hedge ratio for a derivative product, then you know the replicating portfolio, the cost of the replicating portfolio and the minimum price for which you will sell a derivative product—given that the cost of rebalancing the hedge will raise the offering price above this minimum."